MY FISHING YEARS

MY
FISHING
YEARS

FRED J. TAYLOR

DAVID & CHARLES
Newton Abbot   London   North Pomfret (Vt)

British Library Cataloguing in Publication Data

Taylor, Fred J.
  My fishing years.
  1. Fishing
  I. Title
  799.1'2'0924   AH439

  ISBN 0-7153-8105-9

Library of Congress Catalog Card Number 80-85513

© Fred J. Taylor 1981

Typeset by ABM Typographics Limited, Hull
and printed in Great Britain
by Butler and Tanner Limited, Frome & London
for David & Charles (Publishers) Limited
Brunel House   Newton Abbot   Devon

Published in the United States of America
by David & Charles Inc
North Pomfret   Vermont 05053   USA

CONTENTS

To Janet Bonham
for her helping years

ACKNOWLEDGEMENTS

During my lifetime's association with anglers, tackle manufacturers, wholesalers, retailers, journalists, editors and publishers I have made many friends and my fishing years have been the richer for them. All have, directly or indirectly, helped me with this book, and I shall remember them all because this is largely a book of memories. It is not necessary to thank my friends for their friendship, but I do sincerely thank them for their help. They are too numerous to list here, but they will know . . .

I would like to thank Doug Jackson and Marius Pope of the *Standard* for their encouragement over a great many years, and Trevor Bond of the *Sunday Telegraph* for his confidence more recently in my ability.

I would like also to thank John Ingham of *Anglers Mail*, Tony Jackson of *Shooting Times Magazine* and Sandy Leventon of *Angling Magazine* for allowing me a free hand with previously published material—some of which is contained in this book.

I would like to thank Ted Andrews for his artwork, Messrs Heddon of Dowagiac Michigan for permission to use several of their famous fish engravings as chapter heads, and Kevin Clifford for photographic help.

Lastly I would like to thank my American friends for their hospitality and in particular Ted Trueblood of Nampa, Idaho, for his permission to record again his 'Story of the Old Man'. Through him I have learned an even deeper appreciation of the outdoors and how better to enjoy my remaining fishing years.

F. J. T. 1980

9

PREFACE

I have always said my first memory of the waterside is of being tied to a stake while my father, an ardent angler, caught fish on his massive roach pole. Perhaps it is not a true memory but only imagination on my part. Yet, having heard my father tell the story so many times, I have always been able to picture myself on the end of that rope. And I like to think that my introduction to fishing came about that way.

Years later I was allowed to use the two top joints of that same roach pole and to fish with my father and uncle from a boat on Halton Reservoir in Buckinghamshire. I had never actually fished before, but I'll remember that day for the rest of my life. It turned out to be by far the best my father had ever experienced, and, despite having to spend more time unravelling my tackle than he did fishing himself, he never bettered it. My own tally was somewhere in the region of a hundred roach, and the total catch amounted to several hundredweights. From that moment on I was hooked more securely than the fish I caught.

As I grew up, my school holidays and weekends were devoted to scrounging tackle, digging worms, breeding disgusting maggots on dead rabbits, and seeking to catch roach equal to those I'd seen at the reservoir. In those early days I never succeeded, but, with a degree of persistence, I became reasonably competent with a rod. I was not put off by blank days or disappointments, and I quickly learned that there was more to fishing than catching fish.

I would not have seen quite so many of nature's wonders had I not spent so many hours sitting quietly at the waterside. Sadly there are fewer otters today than when I was a boy, but, had I not been an

10

angler, I would never have seen one. Nor would I have had the great thrill of seeing a badger within touching distance as I sat quietly through a summer's night fishing for carp. The hoot of the owl, the great splosh of a leaping sea trout, the brilliance of the swooping kingfisher, the smell of watermint and fresh-cut hay are all part of an angling life. Who cares too much if there are few fish in the net at the end of it all?

And yet there is satisfaction in success.

I found myself answering a challenge, and the urge to catch big fish by design rather than by accident was soon upon me. I picked the brains of others more qualified than I and spent much time just looking and thinking. I never developed great technical skills, but I caught my better-than-average fish by stealth and low cunning. The best tackle in the world will not catch a fish that has been scared into the next county!

I tried my hand at all kinds of freshwater fishing, developing one or two methods that were, at the time, revolutionary. And because I wanted others to know about them, I hesitatingly put pen to paper and spread the word. The outcome of my scribblings was that more doors were opened to me and opportunities to fish other waters came my way. I learned from them all. How to catch fish, but, more importantly, how better to appreciate my weekends and leisure time. My travels in search of fish took me to Ireland, Canada, the United States and Australia. I spent time fishing the Rocky Mountain streams, the lakes of the vast Canadian wilderness and the Australian bushlands. Places where freshly caught fish were essential to survival, but where the act of catching them provided fewer thrills than the breathtaking beauty of the immediate surroundings.

Today I catch trout and enjoy catching them; I still tremble as my float dithers on the oily calm surface of the tench lake, and my heart still quickens when I feel the rod thump in my hand as some unseen pike takes my fluttering lure in the depths of the reservoir.

But more than ever I marvel at the antics of the water vole, the temerity of the robin that takes food from my outstretched hand in winter, the shimmering beauty of the cock pheasant in the morning sun, the mad March hare's cavortings and the wonder of a hatching mayfly. When these things cease to give me pleasure I shall no longer go fishing.

My fishing years have known excitement, drama, humour, sadness, beauty and anger. They have nevertheless brought me great happiness and, perhaps, kept me sane in a world of madness. I have met and enjoyed the company of some wonderful, ordinary people. I have shared their joys and sorrows, and through them I have grown tolerant. I have, from sheer experience, learned that a hundred lifetimes would not be long enough to sample all that fishing has to offer. I once thought I was a knowledgeable angler—skilful with a rod; now I realize how little I really know about the sport of fishing. It comes to everyone in time. Experience helps to improve one's knowledge and ability, but is also very humbling. The more I learn, the more I recognize my own faults and I am embarrassed sometimes at the memory of the arrogance I displayed in years past. I am not alone. Others have felt the same mellowing and tolerance for those who have had fewer opportunities. Wisdom sometimes comes only with experience, and I believe now that I am fortunate to be wise enough to recognize my limitations.

I have shared my fishing years with many people: I would like to share them with others through the medium of this book. But where should it begin?

Perhaps, since I started off as a coarse fisherman and in later years progressed to some of the less demanding branches of angling, it should start with the opening of the season in June, for that is when the coarse fisher is bubbling over with enthusiasm, excitement and anticipation. Was there ever another month like June? And after June will the rest of the year be an anti-climax?

I can only put the pieces together and leave it to the reader to decide.

Fred J. Taylor

JUNE

In June I think of tench bubbles and cruising carp, and I remember how it was when I first began fishing.

F.J.T.

Headstart

Ever since I was a kid and knew that the Yorkshire season opened on 1 June, I had always wanted to go up there to fish on the first day. Eventually the opportunity came.

There were two real reasons for the journey to Yorkshire. One was to meet up again with Kevin Clifford with whom I had fished in America and Ireland, but never in England. The other was to record a carp session with Dick Walker. Timing was critical, and the only available carp fishing we could morally or legitimately pursue on 1 June was to be found in Yorkshire.

Obviously you do not undertake such a venture without a little preparation and consultation, so it was fortunate that we had Kevin as a contact. He not only knew the waters up there, but, being a first-class carp angler himself, knew what to be about in advance. Several weeks beforehand he wrote to say that carp were moving in the swim and that he would 'have 'em crawling up our rods by June 1st'. He had baited down with particle baits (sultanas and corn), and, having had a good deal of experience in that field myself using corn, beans and other seed baits, I felt sure he had the right idea.

13

We travelled up during the day, settled in and prepared to see the night through. It was a coldish night but dry, and the snowmobile suit I brought back from the United States was fabulous. I felt very warm and snug as we sat, 'miked up', under the big brollies talking into the small hours.

There's not a great deal of real work in actually making a recording, but, as I sat there, I thought about all the other work involved. Like Kevin's organizing, in advance, the editing that had to be done later. All Dick and I had to do was talk and, we hoped, catch fish. And I'll say one thing for both of us, we can talk! That is about the only way you can play a game such as this. Scripts and rehearsals are out. The atmosphere has to be real, and after a time you forget about the electronics and settle down to talk naturally. You get off the subject occasionally and often find yourself talking about different fish and different situations that have little or nothing to do with the job in hand. We probably drove our recording engineers half potty, but they were very patient.

Not wishing to load myself down with a great load of unnecessary gear, I took a bare minimum with me and settled for my ultra-light 9ft 3in hollow-glass, touch-leger rod, a few spare hooks and some brand new line. Intending to stay awake all night, I started off using a simple dolly-type indicator rather than a bite alarm. Since I have been using seed baits for carp, I have been inclined to think more in terms of quicker bites and less in terms of generally accepted carp runs. These baits are big enough to fish on substantial hooks, but, because they are much smaller than potatoes or knobs of paste, there is no need to wait for a run to develop. This does away with the need for open-bale adjustment after casting and saves a lot of annoyance. The bale can be closed and the line pulled up taut so that the only slack left is the foot or so where the 'dolly' hangs down. It is a fishing that demands more concentration than the open-bale type, which gives you that little bit of extra time and allows for a certain amount of relaxation. But I suppose it is all a question of mood.

There are waters where bites are so very few and far between that it is nerve-wracking to have to sit poised waiting for something to happen that doesn't. In these circumstances it is probably better to use a bite alarm and sit back waiting for an audible indication. There was, however, no need for that kind of approach on this occasion. Bites (some of them probably false) came quickly, and when Dick, who had been experimenting with some special beta-light floats (high powered and visible at long range) caught the first fish on float tackle, I quickly stole one of them and float fished too. It was the first time I had ever float fished after dark for big carp.

In the past I have often tried to fish with beta-light floats but have generally found them to be useless. Without going into technical details, however, I have to say that those we used in Yorkshire were revolutionary and incredibly effective. My whole outlook on carp fishing after dark was changed overnight.

Dick, I know, wanted to prove a point about them, and he did so to great effect.

I also wanted to prove a point about my little touch-leger rod. It is not the kind of tool I would normally use for carp, but if a rod has to be field tested I believe in subjecting it to some real tests. It is probably a bit unfair, and I know that several of the Yorkshire anglers we met up there were doubtful about the rod's capability, but I felt confident and ignored all advice to use something more substantial.

I lost one fish, but I think I may have lost it anyway irrespective of what rod I was using. The hook hold gave after I had the fish partly under control. But I had no real trouble with the next, a near-thirteen-pounder, despite its several determined rushes towards three different lily beds. A few minutes later I had another eight-pounder.

The next morning we returned six carp to the water, the best of which was a fish of over 15lb caught by Dick.

We were there for another day and night, but we did not fish again. We had done what we had set out to do, and done it solely because Kevin and his mates had cheerfully given up their own opening-day sessions in order to give us as good a chance as possible. When you meet up with that kind of friendly attitude you're rather inclined to forget all about the fishing in order to get to know these people better. Which is what we did.

Despite a first-class fishing session on one of the prettiest lakes I have ever had the pleasure of fishing and the fact that the whole period was recorded, the real highlight came from meeting, talking to, and arguing and theorizing with, those super fellows from East Yorkshire. They were true 'brothers of the angle'.

> *'Surely the very fact that a chap holds a fishing rod means he's a damn decent fellow?'*
> *Gentleman salmon fisher on River Wye to*
> *F.J.T. (who was coarse fishing)*

The Longest Day

What is this magic about 16 June? How does it affect different people? Is it really as 'glorious' as it is reputed to be? Perhaps, now that more and more enclosed waters are being opened up for close-season coarse fishing, and perhaps, now that trout fishing in the big reservoirs is available to anyone who has a fly rod and a day to spend using it, the phrase 'glorious sixteenth' no longer truly applies. Perhaps it is now just another day on the angling calendar and, as such, does not warrant much more than a brief mention. Certainly, it can never mean to our young anglers of the future what it has meant to so many in the past, and that, in itself, is sad.

Sheringham and Chalmers could have put it better than I can, and had Zane Grey fished for tench or carp instead of a big game fish, he too could have put the suspense, excitement and mystery of 16 June into words that only coarse fishers might appreciate. But I will try.

It's a restless day today. You work, and you look at the clock, and you try to concentrate, but it just won't click. You think of the tackle all packed ready, and you wonder if you've forgotten anything. You're on edge all day, and you remember the hours of sweat you've spent dragging the filthy mud and weed from the swim for the past few weeks. You wonder if anyone just might be smart enough, or mean enough, to pull *his* boat out into *your* 'hole' and reap the benefit of your hard work. You worry about the lobworms in the big box in the garage. Are they cool enough; moist enough? Is this sun likely to be too much for them? You wonder if the fish you saw routing around in the swim a couple of nights ago are still there, or if they've cleaned up all the food and moved on to fresh fields. If they have, will it be possible to draw them back? Will things work out this year like they did last year and the year before? Will the weather change and spoil the chances? It's only three o'clock in the afternoon and already there's a gnawing in your stomach; not from hunger but from the sheer suspense of waiting. It will go the moment you're on the boat and safely installed in the swim you've worked on for three weeks, but for the moment life is sheer hell.

You're a tench fisherman and today is 15 June! It is just about twelve hours before you can begin to fish, but those twelve hours will be the longest of your life. Last year's wait *was* the longest; this year it's even worse. You get out into the swim around six o'clock in the evening, knowing very well that you won't be able to fish until, at the very earliest, three o'clock in the morning, and even then you'll be cheating a bit because it's still dark really. You've got a bed-roll and a sleeping-bag (so have your two companions who are in exactly the same state as you), and you know that although you intend to try to sleep, you'll spend all night brewing tea and talking—hoping— wondering. A small fish flips on the surface, and you wonder if it means anything. Are there only small rudd in the swim, or have the tench taken over and pushed the tiddlers out? Was that little surface flipper an odd one, or was he one of many? Is the swim over-fed or does it need some more bait? These and a hundred other worried thoughts go through your mind as you heave aboard the sack of soaked bread, squeeze it as dry as possible by putting it on the bows and 'marking time' on it. Then it goes into the big tub where it is mixed with the fresh

17

oxblood (another cause for anxiety until the man from the abattoir hands over the bucket at the last minute) and dried off with bran and meal. This is the last baiting before the fishing begins. Half of this final, gory mass, which tench love so much that they fairly drool with it, goes into the swim. The remainder stays on the bows until it is needed at dawn.

The night grows cooler, and a mist begins to rise off the water; the bank is no longer visible, but a faint light glows in the darkness, and low voices mingle with footsteps in the distance as a party of bank fishers make their way to the lower lake. They, too, have no intention of being beaten to their swim.

Midnight comes and goes. The lake is still. A moorhen clucks in the rushes. A great fish surfaces and splashes back into the water. It is a long way from the boat, but you speculate as to what it could have been. A carp? A pike? No one will ever know.

You look across to the horizon and remark that it seems to be getting lighter; then you look at your watch and know it isn't! You try to sleep and then begin to worry in case you overdo it and don't wake up in time; but deep down you know there's not a chance! You'll be lucky if you doze for an hour, and you know full well that you'll be exhausted and badly in need of sleep by noon. But you're a tench fisher, and there's nothing you can do about it.

Three o'clock! You can still hardly see your hand in front of your face, but your tackle is made up, and you figure it's as near dawn as makes no difference. In the light of a shaded torch you bait the No. 8 hook with a big lobworm and toss it out into the darkness. You hear it hit the water with a plop, and you tighten up the line in the hope that you might just see the float cock, knowing all the time, of course, that you won't, and being fully aware that you've only tightened up the line so that a good bite from an early tench will register on the rod tip!

Nothing happens. The lake remains still and oily, and daylight still seems far away. A cup of tea might help pass the time, you think, and you reach for the kettle. The rod rattles on the side of the boat, and the tip bends down towards the water. You grab for it wildly, but all goes slack as your fingers close around the handle!

A red haze appears over the tops of the trees on the far bank, and suddenly you can see your float lying at half-cock just a rod's length away from the boat. A second later it has disappeared, but you've done this too many times to be fooled. It's not a bite, just the half-light playing tricks, and you blink the float back into sight again.

It's daylight now, and there's a slight ripple on the water. The white peacock quill rides nicely at half-cock, and the bait lies still on the bottom, anchored down by the one biggish shot that cocks it. The float wavers a little as a couple of balls of ground-bait hit the water close to it. You re-cast and settle down to wait. At last you are really fishing. The three months of waiting, the dragging, the worm collecting, the gathering of bait, the scratching around in brandling compost, the heavy pre-baiting, the soakings, the thick black mud and the piles of foul smelling weed are now forgotten.

You stiffen, hand poised over the rod handle, as the float trembles, lifts half an inch in the water and settles again. You relax momentarily but react almost violently when the float lifts again and falls over flat before gliding away in the manner of a typical tench bite. The rod sweeps back hard and stops suddenly with a satisfying thud as the hook goes home. The reel shrieks a one-second-long protest as you arch the rod to keep the fish out of the thick weed bed, and the cork handle groans as you bend hard to haul it out from under the boat. The tench threshes on the surface, and you lower the rod instinctively to coax the fish to swim deeper. It bores doggedly as only a tench can, and you keep in touch by countering each change of direction it makes. The tackle is sound, the hook is sharp and well set; it is only a matter of time—you hope! Things can go wrong sometimes, however, and, despite your confidence in your tackle, you are cautious with this first fish of the season, but one minute later the mesh of the big net closes round it, and it is safely in the boat.

Fat, sleek, red-eyed, exhausted having fought its heart out

every inch of the way to the boat, it lies there quietly while you remove the hook, guess its weight at about 4lb and slip it back into the water behind the boat.

Nothing's really different. Things are working out about the same as they did last year and the year before. The sun is up now and making white diamonds on the water. There's a smell of watermint from the bank and of bacon cooking in the boat. The kettle's on the boil and the tench are on the feed. It's 16 June again, and for the time being this old world's a pretty good place.

The Brown Bug

'There you are then,' said Ken, 'how about those?' He tipped into my hand a couple of brownish-coloured objects, tied with silk and deer hair, which looked to me like nothing else I'd seen before.

'*Very* nice,' I said, not wishing to appear rude or ignorant. 'Very nice, but what are they supposed to be?'

'Ah well,' said Ken, 'you know when we fish from the boat for those rudd up in Lincolnshire, and we have to keep well back in the boat and throw towards the margins, and you get hooked up in the rush stems and get all bad tempered?'

'Yes,' I said, 'I know.'

'Well,' said Ken, 'perhaps you haven't noticed but, every time the rudd are on feed, there are some peculiar looking brown things crawling about the reed stems. They look something like these things I've just tied. I think!'

'So?' I asked.

'So,' replied Ken, 'I made these things to float, and I figured that next month we might use them with our fly gear, twitch them about a bit and catch some good quality rudd. You might not get caught up so often and carry on so. If you get the right amount of fly line out, you *can't* over-cast can you?'

I saw this point. It was not unusual for me to become over-anxious when rudd fishing, and my attempts to get my bait closer to the rush stems often resulted in my becoming snagged. This did neither the fishing nor my temper any good.

20

It was some time before the new season opened, however, and I thought I might give these particular 'flies' a trial somewhere else—for trout.

I took them to Draycote and caught my first trout of the season on one of them. I was retrieving it quite slowly with short pulls when the trout, a rainbow, took it very decisively.

Next day I caught a rainbow and a brown, and lost two more fish on my remaining monstrosity, which I named the Brown Bug. Then I broke the point off the hook and was left wondering whether or not there was anything special about these flies. Quickly I arranged for Ken to tie me up some more.

At Farmoor a few days later I fished in company with about six other anglers. None of us caught a fish, but I hooked and lost one on a Brown Bug. This time I was hauling it in very quickly as I would a big lure. That was the only offer of the day but it was encouraging.

At Farmoor again, a week later, I fished with Peter Stone, Ken and Tom Rawling, a very experienced trout and sea trout angler. On this occasion I was using a high-density line to get down to the bottom and, after casting, I was allowing the tackle to lie for a couple of minutes before retrieving.

At one stage I cast out the Brown Bug and left it while I had a cup of coffee and a chat with Peter farther up the bank. The chat took longer than I anticipated, and after some time Ken came along and joined us.

'I don't want to worry you Fred,' he said, 'but your rod's thumping!'

I still don't know whether he meant it or not but, when I went back to wind in the tackle, there was a trout attached. I argued, of course, that it had taken while I was retrieving, but no one believed me. I'm still not sure, myself, whether it was on before I retrieved or not.

I *do* know, however, that two days later, back at the private lake, I had a brown trout on a Brown Bug that was definitely not being retrieved. To satisfy myself, I'd made one cast with the hi-D line and left the rod lying on the bank. I didn't take any action until the reel began to unwind!

21

I have no idea whether the fly was still or not, but I am sure that it was not being moved by me, and that, as far as I am concerned, means I was fishing with a static fly. Because of its buoyancy it was probably resting at about mid-water. It is possible that the breeze or something else put some sort of movement into it, but, with 10 yards of hi-D shooting head and perhaps twice that amount of monofilament backing lying on the bottom, I have my doubts. In any case it doesn't matter. What interested me was the fact that the trout took it without any inducement on my part.

The following weekend I was on a small chalk stream with my fly box full of nymphs when I spotted a big trout rising to some kind of surface fly. I had nothing in the way of dry flies with me, but I did have a solitary Brown Bug. It was the only creation I had that would float, and I tied it to my leader. I thought it would probably scare the trout to death, but it didn't. It possibly angered it because it streaked across the pool and hurled itself on to the Brown Bug without a second's hesitation.

I didn't land it. It came off; but it really was a big fish, and I was intrigued.

Four different waters, four entirely different presentations of the same lure, and some sort of satisfaction on each position. It was the answer to my silent prayer. Every trout fisherman has a special, do-or-die, if-this-won't-take-'em-nothing-will kind of lure which he ties on as a last resort. Well now I had one too —the Brown Bug.

It has served me well over the years, but it's absolutely useless for rudd.

Brown Bug Dressing
Ken Taylor

Whip hook shank and tie in a length of nylon at bend of hook. Coat with Vycoat. Use a thin strip of polyethylene for the body, tied along the shank and wound forward to about $\frac{3}{16}$ in short of the eye. Rib with nylon and tie off.

Brown Bug.

The body is then coated with medium oak shellac and top coated with 'Cherry walnut' nail polish, and an equal part of clear varnish. This gives the appearance of a large maggot chrysalis.

A bunch of brown deer hair is spun towards the hook eye to form a collar. This is then clipped close and tapering back to about $\frac{3}{16}$ in long.

Leave a few long hairs from under the collar at the top of the hook to trail backwards.

There are no strict rules about fishing the Brown Bug, as it often responds to unorthodox presentation, and experiment is essential to success.

Hook size: No. 8: whipping silk; brown.

Town and Country

I love little baby ducks
Old pick-up trucks
Slow movin' trains
And rain.

Tom T. Hall
Country-song writer

Anglers are all alike in one respect. They love to stop at bridges and look over into the water. Which, I suppose, is why I take time off to look over Blackfriars Bridge every time I go to one of the big newspaper offices nearby. I never see much except dirty water and garbage, but I look just the same. I suppose in one sense I'm wondering if there will ever be fish in that part of the Thames again. Real fish I mean. Not misleading 'numbers of species', recorded on days when tides have either brought estuarial fish up or freshwater fish down, to have us all believing that the river is now unpolluted.

It was an early June day, and these thoughts were running through my head as I idly watched the pigeons flying around and over the surface of the river. One of the pigeons appeared to drop something into the water, and I watched, puzzled, as a tiny ball of fluff surfaced and began swimming towards a quietly quacking mallard adult. It was one of her young obviously, but I had seen it drop at least 10ft into the water, apparently released by a pigeon. I couldn't believe it, and yet I'd *seen* it!

Suddenly the mystery was solved for me.

Anyone who is familiar with Blackfriars Bridge will know that, running parallel to it, is a disused railway bridge. That bridge is built on iron piles, and those piles are set into great round pillars of brick and concrete. On the day in question the tops of the pillars were about 12ft out of the water, and the 'dome' of one of them was cracked. On the edge of the crack sat another baby duckling trying not to fall off but desperately wanting to do so in answer to momma's calls. Suddenly it began frantically trying to walk around the dome of cement while it plucked up enough courage to make the 12ft dive. Alas, the slope was too much for it, and it tobogganed down at a speed so swift that it shot outwards and downwards well clear of the pillar.

It landed with an audible plop, disappeared for a fraction of a second and then came popping to the surface like a cork. Momma, in the quiet water close to the road-bridge pier, out of the main current, called again, and baby number two joined the great outdoors. He or she was followed at suitable intervals by numbers three, four, five, six and seven. All made the same undignified exit from the pillar and took the same headlong flight into the unknown. Momma then shepherded them all together and moved out with them into the main current. The last I saw of them they were being swept downstream into the distance.

Where they were headed is anyone's guess. What their chances of survival were, I could not begin to hazard, but they must have been considerably higher than my own chances of ever witnessing a similar excursion again.

I have seen (and in my early youth, I'm ashamed to say, robbed) many mallard nests. I have also seen many broods of young ducklings, and it goes without saying that the adult mallard's broken-wing act still fills me with admiration every time I see it performed.

But I have never seen ducklings actually leaving the nest, and I have certainly never watched them executing death-defying dives of 12ft. I had to go into the middle of London to witness such a spectacle and can only marvel at my fortunate timing.

I left the office some hours later to find that the tidal Thames had risen and that the tops of the pillars were now only about 3ft out of the water. The current was turbulent, and the spot where the ducklings had gathered was now a veritable mael-strom. Nothing could have remained still for many seconds in that rush of water, and I found myself wondering just how well that exodus had been timed.

The adult birds had obviously chosen their nest site in the cement crack on top of the pillar. Was it chosen while it was close to the water surface, or at low tide when it was fully exposed? Did the nest-building take place irrespective of tide height with materials being flown on to the site when necessary? And had the parent birds planned for the babies to leave the nest at low tide? Was it all calculated, or was that mallard family extremely lucky?

And there is one more question I would like to ask. Can mallards count? Years ago tests supposedly showed that all birds have limitations and become confused about numbers higher than three. (As an ex-egg-collector in my schooldays I could have told them that without tests.)

So, how did that hen mallard decide that all her young had vacated the nest? Situated as she was, she could not see into the nest, but *immediately* the seventh chick joined her she moved out. No indecision, no hesitation. I watched the nest for another fifteen minutes. I could see part of the inside from my vantage point, and I am in no doubt about it being vacant.

I have thought about that little interlude many times since it happened, and the more I think about it, the more I regard it as the highlight of that year. Not as immediately satisfying as a good catch of fish, not as exciting as a monstrous carp, but really a remarkable experience; all the more so in view of the location.

I know there are many natural phenomena that defy understanding, and I have no intention of trying to answer these questions. Perhaps the whole venture was planned from start to finish; or perhaps it was a whole series of lucky coincidences. I will never know.

But if luck *was* involved, I'd say that most of it was mine for being there to see it all happen.

June's Magic
(Wotton Lakes, Bucks.)

Cold mist rising from the dawn's still water,
Scent of watermint and hay.
Heron's silent lift-off as my footsteps
Sweep away the dew,
And disturb his solitary vigil.
Incessant cuckoo; scampering water vole,
Dabchick, moorhen, turtle dove, and jay,
Make brief protest at my intrusion.

White quill float stands stark against the bulrush,
Slowly lifts and trembles, strives to stay,
But teeters, falls and inexorably dives
Beneath the oily surface.
Tension, pounding heart and trembling hand,
And then, with hour-long minutes passed
Red eye and deep and olive flank of tench.
I hold, admire and then return the first
Of June's Magic.

JULY

In July I recall warm nights by lake and stream, desert sand and mountain peaks, and black coffee at dawn and swallows.

F.J.T.

The Owyhees
From a July Diary

'If hell's any hotter'n this, danged if I don't go git religion!' So spoke a bewhiskered old cowpoke in a Western novel I once read as a schoolboy. It's a phrase I've always remembered and one that I naturally assumed to be one dreamed up by the author.

But it wasn't. I heard it used in the flesh when I picked up my Oregon fishing licence in the local general store—and there was just cause for such a remark. In the heat and dust of that desert country, the thermometer read 108°F in the shade, and I had to agree with the storekeeper who used the expression.

But if that storekeeper thought it was hot there, I wonder what he would think of it here in the desert, on the bank of the vast Owyhee Reservoir? Here, it is 120° in the shade. The temperature of the water is 90° plus and down at 15ft it is still over 80°.

The desert sun shimmers and reflects off the rippled surface and rebounds with an oven-like intensity off the rocks that

27

surround us. Out on the water the boat is so hot that it burns our hands when we touch it. I soak a towel in the warm water, squeeze it out over my head and drape it over my shoulders. A few casts later it is dry again!

Ted Trueblood and I unloaded our camping and fishing gear on to the boat some 30 miles north of here and picked our way up this 50-mile-long canyon to our present camp spot, a small shingle beach with a good supply of driftwood for our fires. It is *not* a luxury camp. We have no shade except that given by the big canvas sheet Ted has erected.

We cook our food in smoke-blackened pans, and at night we unroll our sleeping-bags and lie on them until the air cools down sufficiently for us to crawl inside.

In the daytime the chukars (desert game birds) call and show themselves briefly on the mountainside. They know they are safe for this is not the hunting season. This is fishing time.

At dawn we rise and eat bacon, eggs and frying-pan toast. We wash it down with coffee, hot as fire and black as night; it tastes good. The big, red sun rises atop the craggy peak, and we know it will soon be hot again. But we need fish for food and we have to go to it.

In such a vast expanse of water, hundreds of feet deep in places with no hint of weed or cover, I am lost. I have no idea where to fish, but Ted is wise in the ways of the Owhyhee Desert fish. He knows that crappie abound and that they are eager biters, and he knows where to look for them.

Where the top of the big, flat-topped rock cuts off the sky like a knife, a deep shadow is cast across the water below. On the very edge of the shadow, not in the shade itself or the bright sunlight just beyond, but on the critical edge of the dividing line, at exactly 15ft, lie the crappie. We need no bait and we do not need to cast.

On our fly leader we tie a small lead and above that, three nondescript flies at foot intervals. We lower them over the side and try to arrange for the middle one to settle at 15ft. The rod tip pops and bends downwards, and we set the hook and hold hard. Another pop, and we begin to lift slowly upwards.

These are small fish, and they live in vast shoals, so there is every chance that the third fly will be taken before the first two hooked fish reach the surface. It is fun fishing, but it is also necessary if we want to eat our fill tonight. It doesn't take long to catch all we need, and we spend a few more minutes catching ones and twos and trying for the 'treble'.

At noon we shall fillet them and put them on ice. Meanwhile they are strung deep in the shadow of the big rock, while we take the boat over to the point of the big island to the north.

Here the water is 25ft deep, the bottom is clean, and the temperature is touching 70° at the deepest. This is where the largemouth bass are likely to be, and, as always, the question is 'Will they hit?'

So far they have been dour. A few small ones have been caught and returned, but there has been nothing of note. I wish I could bait-fish like I do in England, but I am told it wouldn't be very effective for largemouth bass here. I tell Ted I *have* caught them on worms elsewhere, but he frowns and tells me not to talk of such things!

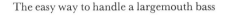

The easy way to handle a largemouth bass

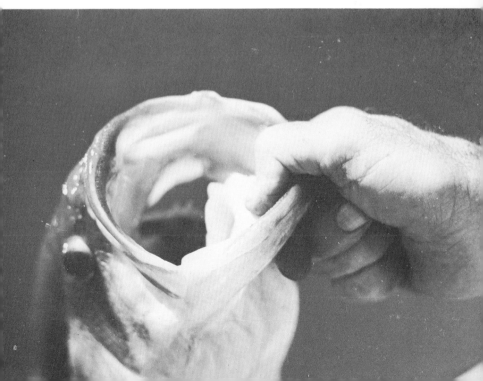

I tie on a hairy plastic worm, a monstrosity as black as coal and armed with a big single hook, and begin bumping it along the bottom. I cast again and again, trying to make the lure take short hops with pauses between each movement. I feel a few plucks, but I am not sure if it is fish or the stony bottom. I strike and miss each time.

Ted hits a two-pounder and turns it loose. I lose one a little bigger and land one weighing about 1lb. The boat drifts into deep water, and we are almost out of casting range, but I make a long, double-handed cast towards the island.

I let the lure sink and then begin winding slowly. There is a sudden stoppage, a surge of power that leaves me in no doubt as to what has happened, and I strike hard.

The fish bores deeply, but I know my tackle and pump him towards the surface. The water erupts, and the bass, for bass it is, hurls itself clear of the surface once, twice, three times, and the reel clutch slips grudgingly as it gives line. Soon it is over, and a huge mouth gulps in air at the side of the boat. I look for the landing net but we don't have one and I panic. Ted laughs.

'Bass are the easiest fish in the world to land,' he says. 'Just put your thumb in its mouth and it comes in like a lamb.' By now I am a nervous wreck and babble at Ted to quit the talking and get the thing in the boat. This is a good fish and I don't want to lose it. But Ted is busy with the camera.

There's no panic he tells me; the fish is hooked well and will not come adrift. I wish I had his confidence, but of course he is right.

We get it aboard and Ted weighs it. Exactly 6lb! My pulse slows down and Ted throws me a can of iced beer from the cooler box. I feel I deserve it, and Ted is obviously more pleased than if he had caught it himself.

We head for camp, picking up the crappie on the way, then light a new fire, brew strong tea and dress out the fish for supper.

After lunch we will fish again, and when the sun has dropped behind the tall hills we will come ashore and eat a meal fit only for those who appreciate this rugged country.

A campsite in the Owyhee country

The Owyhees, Oregon

Eternal desert and relentless blistering sun,
Trail dust, greasewood, sage, gem-studded rock.
Red mountains cutting off the sky,
And towering tall above the Owyhee water,
That spreads itself to lap the desert shore
Where swallows build and quail and chukars call
The night's chill wind stirs up the sand,
And calls for coffee from the camp fire's blackened pot.
The moon holds briefly on a pinnacle of rock,
And, while coyotes talk across the endless void,
I mend the fire, and in its warming glow,
Listen to the changing sounds
Of the West.

JULY

A Lesson Learned

John I'Anson, a Cambridgeshire angler and the only angler I know ever to have caught a burbot, once asked me to accompany him and his friend Hank on an eel-fishing trip. We would go, he said, to a spot on a small tributary of the River Cam where he had previously caught burbot. We would fish for eels with small, dead fish and hope that a burbot would come along too. It was a light-hearted venture, and we expected little more than a pleasant night at the water.

When I arrived at Cambridge that Friday afternoon the sun was hot but, knowing how cold it can become during the night, I put on extra warm clothing before setting out on what turned out to be one of the longest and roughest walks I have ever experienced. Had I known how far it was, I would never have started it, but, encouraged by John's 'It's not far now', I plodded on until we reached a fairly wide and deep sector of a very small river.

It was one of those summers when the ground was a dust bowl and badly in need of rain. A herd of cows came over to inspect us, bringing with them a dense cloud of flies to add to our discomfort. I was thankful when darkness fell, and even more thankful that I'd struggled along with my warm clothing.

Because of the dryness of the ground, worms were unobtainable, and we were forced to use other baits. I had a plastic bag full of dead minnows. They had been caught a couple of days previously and were distinctly 'off' but I was not unduly worried. Eels are seldom particular.

I put two on a No. 6 hook, cast out into the slack and waited —and waited—and waited. No eels, and certainly no burbot condescended to take my bait that night, but I had a rather unusual experience, which taught me something for the future.

At about one o'clock in the morning I had a thumping bite and struck into something that fairly tore off downstream at a terrific pace. No eel this, I thought, and yet I had no idea what it might be. I gradually mastered it and eventually landed a big brown trout just an ounce or so under four pounds! A little

32

later I had a bite from another trout of about a couple of pounds, but this one came adrift just as I was about to net it.

I know trout are greedy, but, if anyone had told me I could catch a big brown trout from that river on *anything*, I'd have been surprised, and if anyone had suggested that I might catch a brown trout on two stinking dead minnows, mounted on a wire trace lying on the bottom of a muddy hole, I'd have laughed myself silly!

Nevertheless, the fact that two trout had taken such a bait in the course of one night proved to me that this was no flash in the pan, and I was to remember it in years to come.

Some of the rivers and lakes I have fished in the United States, for example, are heavily exploited by spin fishermen and bait casters. The trout in these extraordinarily clear waters are not easily fooled, and I remember an occasion when a friend and I were on one of these hard-fished waters and badly in need of fish to eat. There were plenty of trout available, but they would have none of our flies or lures. We were trying to live largely on what we caught, and at one stage it looked as if our camp was in for a lean time; tinned beans are all right in emergencies but they can hardly be called exciting food. When our hopes were at their lowest ebb, I remembered the minnows and the trout back home. I acquired some tiny chub minnows and sat up for a few hours after dark to fish with them. The mosquitoes almost ate me alive, but I ended up with three nice trout, which saved our reputations *and* our stomachs. After two days' hard rations they tasted exceedingly good, and I enjoyed a brief spell of popularity among my friends.

Oh! Those Lonely Nights

I sometimes fish alone on the Cumbrian Esk at night because it is a friendly little river, and I am quite happy without companionship. Elsewhere, I do not care to fish alone after dark. I have tried but do not enjoy it, and I can recall times when I have been very frightened.

The Warrells Lake at Wotton is a beautiful spot by day, but

at night it is transformed into something dark and sinister. I cannot explain why, but I would never think of spending the night there alone. It is quite the most hair-raising water I have ever fished, and I remember that Joe Taylor was always on watch when we fished there together at night. Joe could never sleep and had a strong terror of being left wide-awake while Ken and I slept. It never happened, because, if the conversation ever flagged, Joe would walk over to Ken and me, give us both a kick and say something to wake us up, like 'What time is it?' or 'Any bites?' He continually brewed tea, too, to ensure that, one way or another, we'd be kept awake.

Our three pitches were fairly close together, and we were able to converse in low tones, but on very dark nights it was often almost impossible to see each other.

One particular July night was exceptionally quiet, and, assuming the other two had dozed off, I relaxed in my deck-chair. A strange snorting sound made me look up, and, in the darkness, I made out the shape of what appeared to be an enormous horse standing by the tree a few yards away.

I wasn't scared—just petrified—and, recalling tales of the mounted horseman ghost who rides the estate at night, I stood up and edged my way slowly towards where Ken and Joe were sitting. Joe had meanwhile retired to the little shelter to brew yet another pot of tea and was quiet unaware of my panic. As I backed away from the apparition, Joe soundlessly walked towards me and, mug in hand, whispered in my ear 'Wanna cuppa mate?'

That is the first and only time I have ever executed a vertical take-off! I was scared at Tobruk and Alamein, but never as scared as I was then! We laugh about it now, but it wasn't funny at the time. Joe became scared even though he didn't know why. The horse was probably scared too. It disappeared silently into the night, and we've never really been sure. . . .

It was after that experience, and long after we'd decided that no man in his right senses would spend the night there alone, that we met Philip coming back from the Warrells early one morning! We could not believe he'd spent the night there alone and checked with him to find out if he had done so.

'Oh yes,' he said, 'I often do. It's nice and peaceful and no one bothers me.'

I felt ashamed, but I couldn't believe it.

'You weren't scared?' I asked.

'Nope,' he replied.

'But what about the strange noises and so forth?' I pressed.

'No problem,' grinned Philip. 'I just take out my hearing aid and I can't hear a blessed thing!'

I remembered then that Philip had been rendered completely deaf during the war.

Paradise

*It is exciting to cross the meadows in the early morning.
The swirling mist always hints of good things to come.
The sun may rise too quickly, and that brief hour or so
before it does so may be all too short, but at least the day is
young and there's still a chance.*

Ken Taylor

I have fished many waters for all kinds of fish in many different parts of the world, but if you asked me which one, of them all, has given me the most pleasure, I would unhesitatingly tell you that it was the Warrells Lake at Wotton Underwood. That was my paradise, my fairyland, the water to which I would cycle or even walk, if necessary, in order to try to come to terms with the fine tench I knew to be there. I don't believe I ever failed to catch a tench there during the season, and although I might well have caught more and bigger tench at the nearer Sawmills Lake, I almost invariably chose the Warrells for my all-too-rare weekday fishing trips.

The path to the Warrells was a long and arduous one and it was a struggle to carry bait, ground-bait and tackle across the rickety bridge and along the overgrown tracks to the water's edge. But it was usually worth it. Wotton Lakes were popular, but the long walk deterred all but the keenest of tench fishers, and I usually found that I had the water to myself.

Those thoughts were going through my mind as I pedalled along the main road from Aylesbury and were still with me when I forced my way through the brambles at four o'clock one morning in late July. Arriving at the first summer-house, however, I was astonished and somewhat disturbed to see that two of the swims were already occupied. I had been beaten to it. Not that it really mattered. The swim I wanted, the one by the second summer-house, was still vacant, and I installed myself there quickly in case someone else should have ideas similar to my own.

I had a big bag of ground-bait with me, but when I studied the water I decided not to use it over-generously because there were indications that tench were already present. Big sheets of bubbles were coming to the surface and it was obvious that the fish causing them were very active.

There was a time when I regarded bubbles as a sure indication that the tench were feeding and that it would only be a matter of time before my bait was found and taken, but I had, by then, learned that this was not necessarily always the case. Bubbles almost certainly meant that the tench were feeding, but experience had shown me that they could still be indifferent to anglers' baits. I had spent too many fruitless hours in the past fishing in traditional style with lobworms and paste to be over-confident of these particular conditions.

Fish were bubbling in the other swims too, but none, as yet, had been caught. It was going to be one of those days!

It was to deal with such situations that friends and I had played around with the lift method and developed it into a practical way of catching tench. We gave it its name, but it was a very old method and had been in use long before we ever thought of going fishing.

Despite what has been said in recent years about the lift method, it is still an effective and deadly way of dealing with finicky and unco-operative tench. It suits a muddy bottom and will register bites that are really not bites at all. That is to say, it will give a good indication of when a tench has taken the bait into its mouth, even though it decides to spit it out a split second later. The bottom-only attachment of the float and the critical placing of the shot near to the hook, make certain of this, provided that the whole rig is correctly set. I spent a quarter of an hour or so setting my rig and cutting pieces off my quill float so that the single shot I was using was just heavy enough to sink it. That is the secret of lift fishing. The float has to sink. Sounds strange, but it is a fact.

If the weight of the shot sinks the float, you can be absolutely sure that, when the necessary depth adjustments are made, the bait must be on or very near the bottom. And in the second-summer-house swim, this was important.

There was a slight indentation in the soft muddy bottom just off the point of rushes to my right, and I knew from past experience that this was the hot spot. My bait had to rest in this hollow. A foot to the left or right would have meant fewer bites; probably none at all.

So, by using an over-shotted lift float, which lay flat in water too shallow and sank out of sight in water too deep, I was able at every cast to ensure that my bait was in the right spot. And to make sure that it did not become buried, I used buoyant crust, which hovered just on or above the soft muddy bottom.

A couple of handfuls of ground-bait started the bubbling all over again, and there were slight movements of the float as the tench began to investigate. I cast and rebaited a number of times before I had my first lift bite, but it wasn't too long before I had my first tench, a fish of nearly 4lb.

The crust was washed off the hook many times during the day by the intense activity around the hook-bait area, but each time the float rose up in the water and started to keel over, a quick strike put me into another tench.

I doubt if my bait stayed out more than a minute at any one time. The old and traditional method of leaving the bait out undisturbed just would not work. Catching tench in these circumstances requires the concentration and speed of a match angler. It is no earthly use to sit under a tree waiting for run-away bites. They simply do not come.

On that day it would have been easy to say that the tench

were right off, and that is exactly what I would have said myself a few years previously when I did not know the form.

Fishing the way I did was very far removed from the accepted style of tench fishing. At times my hook was down to a No. 16 and my bait was a piece of crust no bigger then the top of a match. It could truthfully be described as hard work, but I considered it to be worth it. I caught nine tench up to $4\frac{1}{4}$lb.

'You flogged yourself to death,' said one of the other anglers. 'I don't know why you don't just chuck out a lobworm and sit back and enjoy it. The way you fish isn't tench fishing.'

He had caught one tench all day and that remark really surprised me!

AUGUST

*In August I think back to Canada and the wilderness and
catfish and walleye . . . and to sallow bushes and chub and
'cabbages' in the Ouse.*

F.J.T.

The Great Ogoki

I went there to fish, of course, and I caught fish until my arms
ached and my sore bones rebelled, but as usual there was more
to it than just fishing. This was an adventure; a confrontation
with nature in all her magnificent moods.

True wilderness areas are few and far between in this madly
progressing world, but those vast acreages of tall timber, clean
air and pure water in northern Ontario have so far remained
undeveloped.

God's Country they call it; and it would seem that He intends
to keep it that way, for He has made it incredibly difficult for
mere man to exploit.

Deep in the bush, a hundred and more miles from the nearest
road or track, lies the great Ogoki Lake, swelled by the Ogoki
River, which flows north to the Albany and thence eventually
to James Bay.

It appears as but a spot on the map, but in reality its rocky
shores, shadowed by tall pines, spruce and poplars, embrace
several hundred square miles. Beavers work in the deep coves,

39

An Ogoki floatplane

flying squirrels glide between the trees and the haunting call of the loon, that graceful, velvet plumaged diving bird whose survival depends on fish, echoes across the water to break the dawn's silence. Here, a brief flying hour from the nearest access point, time has stood still, and the outdoor lover can find the true meaning of the word 'peace'.

Base camp at Jellicoe lies 760 miles from Toronto, or 1660 miles from New York, and provisions for the week were loaded up after an overnight stay at Jellicoe. The small Beaver float plane took off at eight o'clock in the morning and landed us on Ogoki Lake little more than an hour later. The pilot waved us goodbye, promised to 'see you next week' and that was that! From then on we were on our own!

The camp comprised two rude log cabins and a canvas tent, primitive but adequate cooking facilities, utensils, boats, motors, reserves of petrol and, incredibly in the 96°F temperature, a log-and-sawdust-covered ice bunker! Great cubes of ice over 2ft thick are hacked out of the lake annually in November and remain in this bunker until the end of the summer. Where freshly caught fish are the main source of food and where perishable foods wilt badly in the heat, this ice supply is in-

40

valuable. It even made American beer taste good!

Catching walleyes and pike was so simple that even a non-angler could have succeeded. Small jigs, cast and retrieved slowly across the bottom, were taken enthusiastically time after time, and half an hour's serious fishing supplied our daily food requirements. All fish caught after that were returned alive. Locating the shoals proved difficult at first, but productive areas were soon marked with bottle buoys, and from then on there were no problems.

After several days' exploring the vast lake, and developing man-sized appetites, an American friend (born and raised in that part of Canada and a skilful canoeist and boat handler) and I pushed our way up the Ogoki River to search for white fish and trout. We spent more time struggling over rocks, negotiating rapids and making portages than we spent fishing, but we saw vast areas of magnificent scenery, and I am quite sure we covered ground that few white men have ever trod. I found it an exhausting but unforgettable experience, despite the fact that we caught no white fish or trout—though we still caught walleyes and pike in abundance.

It was nightfall before we made it back to camp and the glow of the log fire guided us in to shore. Succulent fish fillets, caught from the lake the same morning, were already cooking in the great skillet and we, who had existed all day on water from the river, ignored the cook's protests and doubled up the rations! It is always good to eat food cooked over an open fire, and many of our meals were prepared that way, but living in a wilderness camp does not necessarily entail privation. Quite the reverse in fact.

The cabin table was cleared and re-laid daily, and mealtimes were civilized affairs, followed by inevitable washing-up sessions. The propane gas supply fuelled the stove, oven and small refrigerator, and allowed us such luxuries as a turkey roast, biscuits (scones to an Englishman), baked ham and 'walleye au gratin'! Breakfasts daily consisted of bacon, eggs and toast, supplemented by enormous mounds of pancakes and delicious black coffee, made as only Americans know how.

41

A cold-water shave while standing waist-deep in the lake, followed by a soapy plunge, woke us up each morning and another swim in the evening washed away the dirt of the day's activities. But these naked swims had to be well-timed affairs followed quickly by applications of mosquito repellant.

Nowhere in the world are mosquitoes and black flies more aggressive than in the Canadian wilderness! To go into the bush without repellant creams, sprays or lotions is to invite incredible discomfort. To sleep at night without a nearby smouldering smoke coil (available from base camp) is quite impossible, but, if simple precautions are taken, flies and insects need not be troublesome.

Nightly we talked into the dark hours by the light of the log fire, and, though desperately tired, we put thoughts of sleep from our minds for as long as we were able. Camp fires are made for sitting round and talking. They are part of camp life. They give a feeling of security in the wild but, more than that, they give time for reflection.

The smells of young spruce, coffee bubbling in the pot and fresh breezes blowing off the lake, mingle with the pine log smoke; and when the moon tops the tall timbers to add strength to the flickering firelight, it conjures up shadows across the smooth water surface. Only then do you feel the remoteness of it all and pray that these wilderness areas and the creatures that go with them will be allowed to remain undisturbed.

We experienced one electric storm accompanied by torrential rain during our stay. Great thunderclaps shook the ground, hailstones pounded the cabin roof, the fire became a puddle of ash and floating charcoal, a sow skunk and her three babies scurried under the cabin to take up temporary refuge and, just for once, the mosquitoes and black flies were gone!

At its height the storm was frightening in its splendour but, as it abated, I stood out in the warm rain and revelled, while bolts of lightning struck the distant shore.

Storms such as these prevent the planes from coming in, and the possibility of being marooned for an extra day or two is ever present. It is customary to take extra rations to cover this

42

eventuality, which, of course, has to be considered when Atlantic charter flights have to be caught!

Fly-in ventures of this nature need planning in advance. They have their own special problems and timing is important, but somehow they have a relaxing influence from start to finish. Out there in the pines, sleep comes naturally—a sleep induced by healthy exertion and an appetite that has to be experienced to be believed. It really is God's country, but I'm glad to have shared it with Him briefly.

Ogoki Wilderness, North Ontario

Brassy sun burns down upon the great Ogoki,
And spruce and pine and cottonwoods reach upwards from the shore.
Tiny float plane touches down and I alight,
In this vast wilderness where time stands still.
Black flies swarm and flying squirrels glide,
From bough to bough among the timbers tall.
And I seek shelter from the midday sun,
While otters play and loon and whistlers call.
Land of moose and skunk and bear,
Of walleye, pike and speckled trout,
Of pure air and crystal water
That man's progress cannot mar.
God's country this, and He has thus far shown
That so it will remain.
White diamonds sparkle on the water,
'Til black clouds gather, blotting out the sun,
And deluge cools the torrid evening air.
Black flies gone, dust turned to mud
I stand alone and, face turned to the sky,
Accept and revel in the cooling, cleansing rain.
Thunder roars as darkness falls
While lightning bolts attack the distant shore
And I reach out towards the heavens
To embrace this awesome splendour
Of the wildwoods.

Tench and Tradition
From an August Diary

Tuesday p.m. It is almost dark on a warm night, and we are out in the middle of Sawmills Lake at Wotton. We have no intention of fishing until dawn and have spent the last hour or so mixing and preparing bait, making all shipshape and generally preparing for the dark hours. On the bows, another small sack of bread is draining, and later it will be dried off with meal for a final overnight baiting.

The swim is mud-bottomed; it has been well raked and, for the past few nights, fed with a mixture of baits that included brandlings, sweet corn, bread and fish pellets. We have avoided maggots because they almost invariably attract small rudd at this time of year.

I have never been really sure about cross-baiting with several different kinds of food. Some of the old Victorian anglers would never have recommended it, but it depends entirely upon what it is hoped to achieve. Our object has been to encourage tench into the immediate vicinity; if we have done that and then fail to catch them we can hardly blame anyone but ourselves. Had we been trying to 'educate' the tench to one particular bait we would have played it differently.

The cork marker lies about four rod lengths out, and we have planned for the sun (if any) to come up behind us and not dazzle us when it is at a low angle in the morning. Now there is little else to do but wait.

We are out and in position early, and it will be a long night, but with the first hint of daylight we shall be able to commence fishing without delay or disturbance. Anchoring and staking down a boat in the half light of morning is not easy, and settling in overnight avoids scaring any fish that might be in the swim. For me this is not a serious occasion, merely an attempt to re-live old times.

These are my happy hunting grounds, the waters where I learned so much of my tench fishing. I hope to catch fish, but I truthfully do not care too much if I fail. There are so many other attractions, and I have caught tench before. I hope, however, for the benefit of the fellow angler who is my only companion, that the swim produces. I hear the chink of cups as he brews a pot of tea to help pass away the long vigil.

Deck-chairs are set on their lowest notches, warm clothing is ready to slip on when the night air chills, the landing net is made up, and there is a big keep-net available if we are lucky enough to want to keep a specimen or two for weighing. Eric has dried off the ground-bait, and half of it is now going into the swim. The big old cob watches us from a distance, but he is not interested in the bread. His mate is still fussing over her cygnets nearby, and he is merely standing guard.

A few pond olives are hatching, and small fish are flipping on the surface; a coot 'clinks' in the reed mace, and two mallards home in on the nearby island. It is almost dark now. The night air chills and it is time to pull over the canopy and snatch a few hours' sleep.

Wednesday p.m. I woke up to the sound of splashings near the boat and, when I finally got things into focus, I saw Eric lift up the landing net to reveal a nice tench of about 3½lb.

'I couldn't sleep,' he said, 'and you were well away, so I left you to it. You never heard me lift the canopy and bait up, and I was about to brew some tea and waken you when I had this bite—see. I missed it, and several more—on lobworms—so I put on a bit of crust and here is the first one of the day.'

I made a pretence of being cross about sleeping on but, in fact, I was really glad of the extra hour. Eric was too busy tench fishing now to worry about such minor things as brewing up, so I took care of it myself.

It had rained in the night and the bows, stern and canopy were still wet, but the inside of the boat was bone dry, and, as the sun rose behind the canopy shade, I began to peel off some of the warm clothing I had worn through the night. Surprisingly I had woken up once during the night feeling decidedly chilly despite great layers of insulation; but it can be cold on an exposed lake at night. How anyone manages to survive in an open punt I cannot imagine, but some do and seem to thrive on it. My answer to the cold was to close the canopy over completely and light-up my small gas camp stove. In minutes the whole boat was warm again, and I felt capable of seeing the night through.

By now, however, the sun was being wasted on the canopy behind us, and I lowered it to take advantage of its warmth.

With my spirits restored by strong tea and weak sunshine, I made the effort to fish seriously for a time and to try to catch up with Eric, who had since put two more tench in the keep-net. My heart was not in it. I was not out for blood. I intended to fish the old-fashioned way as I did when a boy with a big bait, hard on the bottom and a float at half-cock, waiting for a bite that pulled it out of sight. A lazy way of fishing, a way that does not keep up with modern developments, new float designs and present-day techniques, but at least it has one thing going for it —tranquillity. I am reminded, every time I practise it, of Sheringham's lovely passage.

> Having laid out your rods (you may just as well use two while you are about it, with a different bait on each) you are at liberty to smoke, meditate, read, and even, I think, to sleep. You and the rods and the floats gradually grow into the landscape and become part of it.

I doubt if you could read or sleep with any real chance of seeing a float go under, but it is true about becoming part of the landscape. Even in a boat, staked down in the middle of the lake, it still applies, if the mood is present. I am glad that I can still revert to that kind of mood occasionally.

I do not *always* want to sit poised over a rod ready to pounce every time the float twitches. I do not *always* want to keep casting and re-casting, baiting and ground-baiting in a frenzied attempt to extract a maximum from the swim. I can do it, and very often, when I am in that kind of mood, I enjoy the challenge; but how I would hate to do it all the time!

Many tench anglers have not enjoyed their day if they have not had a great haul, and for that reason they fish hard and go home exhausted. I am not in any way against their attitude.

46

I once held similar views myself. These anglers enjoy it that way, and that really is the essence of fishing, but I am very glad I can see it differently and derive my pleasure from tench fishing in so many different ways. Bloody-minded efficiency does not always give me the maximum pleasure.

So I sat there, experimenting with big hook-baits made up of brown bread and fish pellets, trying to prove a point if possible, but caring little one way or the other. It is an attitude that has to be developed if the object is to experiment with baits, and today I found it easy to disregard all but the beauty around me.

Eric's final tally was seven tench, all between three and a fraction over four pounds. Mine amounted only to a brace of four-pounders, but I had done what I wanted to do, which was to catch some tench from my chosen swim and find out something about a new bait in the process.

While we packed up, Eric, who was delighted with his bag of fish, threatened to offer proof, at odds of seven to two, that he could outfish me any time.

What he doesn't know, bless his heart, is that I was never disputing it anyway.

Road Hawg

The heavens opened at midnight, and a great sea of water emptied itself upon the sleepy little town of Hanna City. Thunder boomed and lightning crackled in thirty-second-long bursts across the black skies of north Illinois. Hailstones the size of walnuts hammered down on the roof shingles, and the residents, myself included, forgot about sleep and waited for the dawn. When it came the deluge and the din had ceased. All was quiet, but chaos remained in the form of ripped-up rail tracks, washed-out bridges and flooded basements.

The town was a sorry sight, but there is very little you can do about a flooded basement, except wait for the water level to drop, so Jack Ehresman, my brother Ken and I decided not to deviate from our original plan, which was to go fishing. Perhaps the basement would dry out in the meantime!

We went fishing, but it was only a gesture. In water the colour of chocolate malt, a bass could hardly be expected to see a lure and, with its gills choked with mud, it would show little interest anyway. After half an hour of negative going-through-the-motions, we retired to the cabin, opened a bottle of sour-mash bourbon, and began telling fishy tales and lies to each other.

Meanwhile, the dam holding back the mile-long lake in the hills above us was feeling the effects of last night's storm. It held until afternoon, but eventually its saturated soil crumbled and finally burst under pressure from the excess water.

A great cauldron emptied into the gorge, pushing clay boulders in front of it, ripping out grass and bushes in its wake. The water flowed round the hill and backed up towards the cabin silently and unnoticed, while the level of the bottle lowered and we waxed more eloquent.

'It was on this very road out here,' said Jack Ehresman, 'that I stopped the car a couple of years ago to let a big old hawg of a carp swim across the road.'

Road-runner carp

That, I thought, must be the medal-winner! I treated the story with the contempt I felt it deserved, but Jack swore, hand on heart, that it was true.

At that moment I spotted the water creeping up to the cabin door and, looking out, saw that we were isolated from the road and completely surrounded. Another inch and we'd be awash so, wet feet or not, we made for the car and drove towards higher ground. Around the bend we came to a halt. The small spillway, unable to cope with the greatly increased flow had breached, allowing floodwater through the fence across the road. (We learned later that this breach actually saved our cabin from further flooding.)

And I swear to you that, before my very eyes, a big old carp flopped his way across the granite chippings and disappeared in the flooded meadow beyond! It was followed by another, and a third that somehow or other managed to fight its way back through the breach and find the sanctuary of the flooded osiers higher up the bank.

Up against the wire fence I spotted a movement and, walking closer, saw yet another carp, this time high and almost dry, wedged against the mesh where the rush of water had deposited it earlier. It was still alive and, while its life meant nothing to Jack, I felt the urge to rescue it, to give it a chance; and so with shoes and socks removed I freed it from the wire. A fast flow of clean water was now coming through the breach and I held the fish in it until it revived. It was completely unharmed, and I felt pretty good about the whole thing. So much so that I nursed it in the car's front seat while Jack drove back towards the cabin where I'd decided to release it in the quieter water.

'Hell no, you can't do that,' said our host, Leroy Larsen. 'That's a good eating fish and I've got a friend who loves 'em. Put it in the live well on my dock.'

Leroy has a boat dock (which by this time was a foot under water) and below it is a deep cage where he keeps fish alive until they're required for eating. There was room for a dozen fish like the carp I held, and it would have been perfectly safe in that quiet prison, but it grieved me to think I'd been to all that trouble for nothing; that my carp would only live until someone knocked it on the head and put a fillet knife through it!

I struggled with the bolt on the cage door with one hand, grasping the carp firmly under my other arm, watched closely by the other three who offered plenty of advice but no assistance. It was obvious that they had no intentions of getting wet and that they reckoned one wet-legged fool in the cabin would be enough.

The green moss on the boat dock, now soaked and slippery, squelched between my toes as I opened the trap door, and, at that precise moment, the carp came back to life. My feet slipped from under me, I grabbed for the dock rail to keep my balance, and the carp—all ten or eleven pounds of it—sailed gracefully over my head and landed with a great splosh in the open water, where it made a dignified escape.

I have experienced a number of soakings when trying to pull a fish out of the water, but that was the only time I was ever soaked trying to return one.

Stink-bait

I first fished for channel catfish and brown bullheads in Canada in 1967. I caught my best ever there from Georgian Bay, and I'll remember the fight of that ten-pounder for all time.

I wanted to catch catfish again, of course. Who wouldn't, having once caught and eaten them on the same day?

I went to Idaho in August some years later as I remember, with a view to seeing the western states and fishing for trout, bass and crappie, but when I heard there were catfish a-plenty around, I asked my host Ted Trueblood if we might have a try —just once. He agreed. He wanted me to have fun, and both he and his lovely wife, Ellen, were enthused about a catfish supper. I was glad of the opportunity but made it clear that I didn't really want to wait for big fish (although, naturally, I hoped one might show up). I just fancied sitting quietly in the darkness catching some nice fish for eating.

Ted reckoned he knew such a spot on the Snake River in

American-style stringer of
channel catfish and bullheads:
a meal for two campers

Idaho, and he took me to it one night. The water below the big
hydro-electric installation was fast and turbulent, but there
were slacks and eddies, which looked inviting. It was, however,
a vast expanse of water, and I was really at a loss how to fish it.

I had some worms (which in this desert country with the
temperature in the lower hundreds was really a great achievement), and I settled for a 1oz leger-rig, similar to the one Ted
himself used. I baited up, cast into the darkness and waited.

I was suddenly aware of an absolutely disgusting smell behind
me and, thinking that it came from the hydro-electric installation, asked Ted what it was they were discharging.

'Discharging?' said Ted. 'Hell, that's my catfish bait!'

I'd heard of these so-called secret 'stink-baits' for catfish, but
I'd never been so close to one before, and I was rather sorry
that I was just then. I simply couldn't describe it except to say
that it was vile.

I suppose the basis was cheese, but what else it contained I
couldn't hazard a guess. It was about the consistency of syrup
and needed very careful handling.

51

What you did, apparently, was bait your hook with a piece of foam rubber, leaving the point and barb exposed. Then you dunked it in the repulsive 'goo' and poked it around with a stick until it became saturated.

'That,' said Ted, 'is the damnedest catfish bait ever invented. It's full of nourishment; the catfish love it and it really doesn't smell half as bad as you're trying to make out.'

I poked around with the stick with my head turned to windward. 'Sweet as a nut,' said Ted, and then: 'Don't get any on the outside of the jar, I've got to put that back in my tackle bag, damnit.'

I sneaked back and had a look at it a couple of times, especially as Ted seemed to be catching fish all the time, but I couldn't face it. I stuck to worms and caught very few fish compared with Ted. We went home with a full stringer at about two o'clock in the morning.

A few days later Ted suggested that we might have another session in a spot nearer to home where the water was not so turbulent. I agreed, of course, and then, too late, realized that

A brown bullhead (catfish) from Oregon

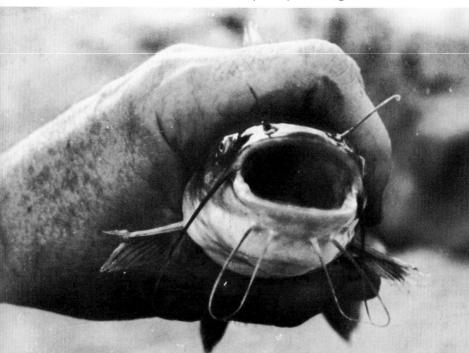

I was out of lobworms. Ted already had the gear in the car, and I groaned as I saw him come out of the garage with another big jar of stink-bait. I was, to use an English expression, lumbered!

I liked the look of the river. It was almost as fast as the Hampshire Avon and seemed more like the waters I'm used to fishing at home.

I experimented a bit with leads and finally found that a $\frac{3}{8}$oz bullet held nicely. Later, I changed to a swanshot link-leger of about the same weight to avoid tackle losses.

Ted used the same big bullet he'd used before and argued, reasonably, that, as the line passed through it, there should be no need for line adjustments regarding the casting weight.

I explained the theory of light legering and convinced him that there are situations where the angle of the line in relation to the current is such that the lead itself moves, or tries to move, when a fish bites.

If the lead is too heavy in these circumstances it could, and often does, result in missed bites. A lead that just, and only just, holds bottom, will move at the slightest touch and register at the rod end with less chance of the fish feeling resistance. My lighter leger did just that and my results were decidedly better.

Yes, I managed to steel myself into using the stink-bait, and after a time I found out a little about fishing with it. The bites were different from anything else I had experienced, and I found that the catfish almost invariably tried a preliminary taste before picking up the goo-soaked sponge.

Ted said that they were just 'sampling the lovely goodies' and that they could, on occasions, squeeze all the 'nourishment' out without ever running off with it. Sometimes they did, but mostly, after a couple of pecks, I felt the slow pull on the rod tip, which I usually managed to hit. It was really like barbel fishing in the dark.

That night we had twenty-nine catfish, and I had probably twice as many as Ted. I certainly had more bites, and I should also add that there was a time when I was fishing and Ted was busy filleting.

I suppose we both stank to high heaven, but somehow we seemed to get used to it as time went by. 'I can't smell it on you,' said Ted, 'and you can't smell it on me, and that's how it should be. Dammit, ten polecats can live in the same hole for a year and not complain, so why should we! Even so, I guess we'd better take a bath!'

That was a great night, and I was very pleased that Ted, who normally loves to fly fish and bait-cast for bass and trout, was prepared to sit and bank fish with me. I learned, however, that he is no game-fish snob. Fishing is fishing, and he uses the methods most likely to catch the species he is seeking.

Even when we were out in the desert, boat fishing for bass and crappie, Ted would join me after dark and fish for the delightful little bullheads that abounded in the huge lake. They

FJT being presented with the Silver Dolphin Award in Atlanta, Georgia, where he was installed in the International Fishing Hall of Fame in 1978

were fish of, perhaps, a pound, and we took them on little pieces of fish meat and super-light, soft-actioned casting rods. On that gear they fought like demons. We kept a few to eat but returned most as we caught them.

The bullhead has a really large, whiskery mouth, much bigger than that of a channel catfish, and I'm fond of him because he doesn't care for stink-bait at all.

There's little doubt in my mind that, as far as bait fishing goes, our English legering techniques are better than those used by the average American, but they are truly unnecessary. In a country of unsophisticated fish, there seems to be no need for the finesse we regard as essential in England. Our fish have learned, but the fish in the remote American waters seldom have the opportunity and, as a rule, they're easy to catch.

I have occasionally caught both channel catfish and bull-heads since those early days, and I have never tired of them. Opportunities come all too infrequently, since most of my American friends are not interested in bait fishing. I cannot really say that I blame them, if bait fishing means putting up with evil-smelling concoctions. There surely must be other ways of catching catfish! When I boarded the plane at Boise and waved goodbye to Ted, I could still smell that awful cheese-like potion. It lingered all the way to Chicago and on to Springfield, Illinois. Imagination, of course. But why did the lady sitting next to me get up and move to another seat?

And why were my friends in Jacksonville a little less anxious to embrace me? And why did my own dear wife screw up her nose and ask me where on earth I'd been?

There was a yellow blob of stink-bait on the shoulder of my shirt, placed there, quite by accident I'm sure, by that enthusiastic and expert fisherman, Ted Trueblood. I have since forgiven him!

Fish and visitors stink after three days!
Benjamin Franklin

Klon

Down by the little red bridge, on the road that led to the big estate, the roach shoals were patrolling back and forth over a long stretch of the little river. When you could see them thus you could never catch them. That was a known fact. Even the old hands knew that fishing then was a waste of time and that you had to wait for dusk, or else come again at dawn. It wasn't because the fish could see you, it was because they were 'off the feed'. We knew all about it. We'd waited time and time again for the shoal to pass by and dropped our floats in at the precise moment, allowing the white pills of paste to sink enticingly in front of the fish, but it was no use. They weren't interested, and you couldn't do anything if they weren't feeding. So we gave it up and went to climb trees and swim. Before we went, however, we baited our tackles and threw them out to fish by themselves close to the dark green reeds. Up by the bridge, the water was some ten feet deep, and in summer we used to dive off the old brickwork and become temporarily preoccupied with salvaging from the bottom rocks that we knew to be part of an earlier bridge that had collapsed a hundred years previously. That may have been an exaggeration on our part. Schoolboys tend to have rather vivid imaginations, but the rocks were there, and the water was warm, and the fish weren't biting anyway. So, why not?

The white-haired old gentleman with the big bundle of rods and a wooden fishing-box clambered down the bank and walked on downstream past our set rods. He stopped every so often and looked into the river, shading his eyes from the sun with his hands. We knew he was watching the shoals of roach, and we knew that, like us, he wouldn't be able to catch them either. We carried on swimming and forgot him.

An hour later we went back to our rods and, wonder of wonders, each hook held a lively, kicking roach. Some fish, at least, were feeding despite the heat and bright sun. (Did it ever rain when we had holidays from school?)

Downstream there was a splashing on the surface. The old

gentleman lifted out a half-pounder and laid it on the bank with a dozen others of the same weight. We grabbed our rods and made a take-over bid!

It is to his credit that he did not throw the pair of us in, but perhaps he thought it wouldn't have bothered us anyway. We spent as much time in the water as out of it those days. He was not even angry—though in truth he should have been. He left us strictly alone while we fouled up his chances of catching any more fish and then called us over to him. He was standing well back from the water's edge and hidden from the fish by the tall rushes.

'If you want to catch fish, boys,' he said, 'you've got to fish long and light. Sit quietly for a while and I'll show you.' We sat!

He picked up his enormous pole, baited his hook with a piece of bread paste and lowered it into the water. The tiny porcupine float moved down slowly with the current, quivered momentarily and disappeared from sight. The old gentleman twisted his wrist, the line tightened, and a glistening, silvery shape came swinging across the rushes. 'There,' he said, 'see what I mean?'

We watched him do it again and again and again. He wanted no more fish for himself but he offered them to us, but we refused politely because we were not fond of the roach from the little river. We liked the perch. We took the roach as he caught them, however, and returned them for him downstream away from his swim, but all the time we were eyeing his bait. It was special, we said. It contained something different. Well it *looked* different because it was golden coloured and not white like ours.

'That's just because I leave the crust on,' he said. 'Here, try some yourself.' We tried some and once again failed to catch fish.

'Give me some of your bait,' said the old gentleman later when things had quietened down and we were seated with him away from the water's edge again. We gave him some and he proceeded to catch fish once more. We were dumbfounded and somehow could not seem to understand why he could do this.

57

To us it was little short of magic. We thought of a hundred excuses and reasons for his success and our failure, but he just chuckled.

'Long and light,' he said. 'Or, if you like, fine and far off. You'll never catch roach like these by fishing on top of them. You've got to keep back out of sight. Here let me show you. Take a hold of this pole.'

He handed me his pole and, though I grasped it with both hands, I could not hold it steady. So he removed the bottom joint and handed me the shorter version. 'Now,' he said to my friend Frank, 'you stay here, and watch.' And to me he said 'You creep forward and drop the float in the water, like I've been doing. Only *keep out of sight!*'

It wasn't easy for me, and I suspect it was even harder for Frank to watch, but I did as I was told, and I caught a roach very quickly. Frank took a turn, and he too caught a fish on the shortened pole.

The old gentleman was very strict. He let us each catch one fish before handing over the rod and, although he took a turn himself occasionally, he spent most of the time advising and keeping us in check. We learned a lot that day.

It is now many years since that old gentleman, whose name was Klon, died. He was over ninety and completely blind, but he still remembered, and so did I.

'Is that you, young Jimmie?' he'd say. He always called me Jimmie after my father, whom he knew well.

'Yes Klon,' I'd say. 'It's me.'

'Remember when I taught you how to catch roach, Jimmie?' he'd say. 'I showed you a thing or two that day didn't I?'

And I'd say, 'Yes Klon. You showed me plenty.'

And I meant it.

SEPTEMBER

In September I think of sea trout and eels and barbel and the coho of mighty Michigan . . . and camp fires on the Rocky Mountains and cut-throat trout and brookies and blue jays and pine squirrels and a long journey.

F.J.T.

Alders casting eerie shadows, adding to the mystery,
Of the deep and rocky pool.
Chuckling waters from the shingle run,
Surge round me as I cast into the darkness,
Intent on leaping sea trout, but remaining still aware
Of hooting owl and rustlings from the creatures of the night.
Dawn's first gleam and sudden understanding,
That, all too quickly, night has gone.
Sleepy pheasant clucks and startled rabbit scuttles,
As I leave with heavy eyes and memories,
And thoughts of sleep and new nights yet to come.
The sunrise builds an orange fire above the crag
And while the valley wakes,
I ease my load to rest a while,
Lest the magic of this moment
Should, too swiftly, pass me by.

Lean Times

In anticipation of a long-awaited visit to my favourite little northern river, I had let my memories wander somewhat and allowed my pen the luxury of the descriptive passage that heads this chapter.

I still have vivid memories of the 'fire above the crag'. No other dawn was ever quite like it. There was one occasion, however, when I saw my orange fire in the middle of the afternoon: the whole fell was burning following a prolonged drought.

Brother Ken and I were interested in water rather than fire, however, and, although we expected to find the river low and clear, we were hoping for conditions a little better than we found. In all the years I have fished there, I have never seen the situation so depressing, and I knew at once that our chances of fresh-run sea trout were precisely nil. But we had made a long journey, put a lot of time and effort into our plans, and as we had come to fish, we did just that—in pools that were apparently devoid of fish.

It was quite easy to see every rock, every pebble—almost every grain of sand—in the crystal-clear water, and, had we not known a little of the habits of sea trout in these conditions, we might have written the pools off as hopeless. But under the big rocks we knew fish would be hiding, resting, sleeping or whatever they do during the daytime, and we sat and watched. Every so often the dark shadow of a fish would slide from one rock to another. A grey shape would appear briefly and drop back. Here and there an odd tail showed from under the rocks, a flash of silver betrayed the presence of a single herling. It was not a rosy picture, but at least there were a few fish present, and we had worms by the hundred.

Fishing these rocky pools at night with worm tackle is, in my opinion, the most difficult of all angling methods. Certainly I have never practised anything more demanding anywhere else in the world, and I knew that, because of the lack of flow, it would be almost impossible to be really efficient in the darkness.

With just the slightest pull on the water, it's possible to *feel* what the worm is doing, where it's travelling, how it's behaving. With virtually no pull at all, it became necessary to free-line and *try* to keep in touch with the slowly sinking bait. It's a non-stop procedure. There is no easy way out. You cannot cast, let the bait sink and sit back to await results, because you will simply end up by being snagged in the rocks. The bait has to be kept clear and gently on the move, by sheer feel; and that is not easy. With a current you can ease it over obstructions and keep it working; with no current at all the movement has to be put in at the rod end. You have to feel for the slightest pluck with the line between your fingers, and this means that, after casting, the bait has to be drawn back by hand—slowly.

In the darkness, a 6lb line is quite invisible, and this gentle drawing action inevitably allows a certain amount of slack to accumulate near the reel. It only needs one turn to wrap itself around the bale, and the result is an unbelievable mess, which has to be taken well away from the water and sorted out by torchlight. Ken and I have overcome that obstacle in the past by taking hold of the line *above* the butt ring before imparting the movement. It helps, but it is by no means guaranteed.

Then, of course, there are the eels. It takes an eel about twenty seconds flat to locate a static worm on the bottom, and on the odd occasion when we relaxed and let the tackle fish for itself, that is what we caught. Eels are fun, if they're fished for properly and if they're of useful size. These range from 6in bootlaces to 12in slimy horrors that ball the tackle up into an impossible heap. All you can do is break off and tie on another hook; and after five or six such occurrences you start to wonder if it's worth it.

Then, suddenly the pool becomes alive with leaping, splashing fish, some small, some enormous; and you take heart once more because you know that there's just a slender chance. After another couple of hours without so much as a knock, you begin to realize just how impossible sea trout can be, but you accept it as part of the game and continue. If the moon comes up, it makes life a little easier but almost certainly reduces the

Silver Creek, Idaho: who cares about fishing in surroundings like this?

odds even more, and later, as it shines across the glassy surface, all activity ceases and you know, deep down, that it's time to catch up on some sleep.

Ken and I played it that way for a couple of sessions with no success before deciding to try using luminous floats.

What would happen, we wondered, if we let the baits dangle just clear of the rocky bottom out of the way of the eels? We tried, and that's just about all that *did* happen. The baits dangled and the floats remained motionless. So much for that smart idea!

And then, some two hours later, Ken's float slowly, purposefully disappeared from sight, and he was into a sea trout that ripped off line, leapt with a great splosh at the head of the pool, then turned and tore off downstream.

I grabbed the net, scrambled to assist him, stumbled, fell and cracked my cheekbone on a great rock. I didn't actually pass out, but I knocked myself half silly, and it was a minute or so before I could get myself back into focus. I handed Ken the net, and the fish came off the hook 6in from it at full stretch. Night fishing for sea trout is not only difficult but positively dangerous.

Part of our pleasure in these wild places comes from catching enough fish to eat and survive, but these were lean times, and the larder was almost bare.

A most frustrating experience

'Why don't you go,' said Hugh Falkus, 'to the tiny beck where you caught all those little wild brown trout a couple of years ago. They're good fun to catch and especially good to eat with bacon for breakfast as you well know.'

And so, with tiny fly rods, a few worms and maggots, we made our way across the fell to the little beck. We were full of heart but, alas, the beck no longer existed. It was just a dry, dusty ditch, and our disappointment was not helped by the fact that our long walk had given us enormous appetites. Half a dozen plump little brownies could have taken care of them very nicely, but it was not to be. All was not lost, however. In a lower pool on the main river, a few herling and small sea trout were showing. We scared them as we approached, but they returned once we'd settled in to fish from behind cover. Then began one of the most frustrating experiences I have ever endured.

We were able to see every fish in the pool and watch their different reactions to the delicately presented, free-lined worms. How many hours we spent, utterly fascinated, I couldn't try to guess. Time simply stood still as fish after fish moved towards the baits without taking. Sometimes the worm would lie wriggling in full view on a flat-topped rock with one, two, even three sea trout eyeing it with suspicious interest. Sometimes the slowly sinking worm would actually touch a resting fish without provoking any reaction. Occasionally a better fish would make an irritated swipe at it as it dangled motionless near the bank. At times there would be no fish visible at all, and then, seemingly from nowhere, they would begin to reappear. Finally, one of them picked up my worm and swam off with it, holding it lightly by the tail with no intention of ever taking it. There was no point in striking; I could see the hook was nowhere near its mouth, and I waited hoping for it to disappear inside. It didn't, of course. The fish spat out the worm, then took it by the other end, turned over on its back, shook it like a terrier shaking a rat and finally gave me back the middle portion.

Several times it happened, several times I thought I might be in with a chance, and once, when I could stand it no longer, I tightened. That fish never came back.

Meanwhile Ken was having exactly the same problems, and with hunger really taking hold of us now, we scaled down and fished with a couple of maggots. One BB shot was all we dared to use, and with a long trail the bait sank slowly and fairly naturally to the gin-clear pool.

Suddenly Ken was into a fish and our prospects of breakfast began to look brighter. It was only a half-pound herling, but what a difference it made to our hopes. Between us we caught a dozen of them, and, as I recall, we ate breakfast at three o'clock in the afternoon. Never was a late breakfast so hard won or so deeply appreciated. We demolished six of those fish and saved the rest for supper but, understandably perhaps, we fed no more for the rest of the day.

Over the three days our total catch comprised but two dozen herling and small sea trout. A poor result for two anglers by normal standards but, we were assured, remarkable in the circumstances.

The most interesting part of all our daytime fishing was the fact that we could actually watch a single maggot lying in 7ft of water and see exactly whether or not a fish had taken it. A thousand times after settling, the bait would be nosed, nudged, inspected, sat on, sucked in and rejected in a split second, or ignored completely.

Two maggots were regarded with obvious suspicion and refused entirely. A single maggot on a No. 16 might be accepted with luck, but all too often the 2lb hook link seemed to deter the fish. That, or they could see or sense the hook in some way.

These were small fish, and their size did nothing to cause any real excitement; but their nearness and their awareness set me trembling more than many fish ten times their size might have done.

The climax to my last session came when I scaled down to a No. 20 hook and a 1lb link to fool the biggest fish I could see in the pool. It was a mere one-pounder, but after an age of inspection and a hundred refusals, it casually sucked in the bait and swam off with it. Playing it cautiously, as I had to in the circumstances, caused panic among the other residents, and, when Ken finally netted it, the pool appeared to be empty once more.

For three days we'd hoped for rain, and for three days the sky had remained brassy with the sun scorching the surrounding land. There was no hope of improvement, and so we began the long task of packing and re-loading the car. At which stage the deluge began! Two more days and the spate, which was surely on the way, would have subsided. The river would be full of fish fresh-run from the sea, and we might have enjoyed a sea trout bonanza, but our time was up and we had to leave. The best laid schemes. . . .

As we drove off the downpour doused the flames on the fell, and the crag, spouting smoke like an angry volcano, retained its magnificence in a different kind of way.

Colour was creeping into the river as we crossed the bridge, and as we pushed on through the rain and darkness, we talked of what might have been and wondered about the future. The little river had been harder than usual but it had never been unkind.

> *The hill tops are tipped with gold. Through the trees there is a glimpse of distant hay fields. Under the pink clouds, larks are singing; a white ribbon of mist lifts from the water meadows, and high against the fell side, the cottage windows glitter with early light.*
>
> *Sit awhile to breathe the morning freshness and catch the beauty of the sunrise.*
>
> Hugh Falkus

Eels and Ills

There is a spot below the fishing hut on the River Test where the keeper cleans all the salmon caught. The salmon roe and offal that find their way into the river attract eels, and it is only necessary to cast in a bait, lean the rod against the fence and wait for it to turn a full quarter circle to catch eels there by day. I always had a yen to try it at night, however, and on one fine September Saturday the dream became reality.

I can never take eel fishing terribly seriously, and I confess this was a fun trip pure and simple, but on reflection I know that we should have given it more thought, that we should have treated it as a one-off venture and that it ought not to have been tied in with a trout-fishing trip at the same time.

Gerry Hughes, of *Anglers Mail*, joined Ken and me down on the trout stream in the middle of the afternoon, and between us we caught six nice fish, including a five-pounder. It was a warm day, ideal conditions for eels, and, knowing this, we should have made our way to the eel swim earlier, but we relaxed over tea and sandwiches (and, I regret to say, the best part of a bottle of sour-mash Kentucky Bourbon, which the river keeper encouraged us to imbibe) and got off to a late start.

For a start, Gerry, who had told us on the 'phone not to worry about bait because he had plenty of worms, forgot to bring them. This created a small problem, since it is rather difficult to catch eels without bait, as most anglers would know.

However, the six trout needed dressing out, and, after cleaning them, I kept the guts, livers and gills for bait. Most of the guts went in well in advance as ground-bait; I kept back the livers and gills as hook-baits.

Fish gills have an attraction for a number of fish, not excluding perch, but they appear to be particularly attractive to eels. I had had this thought in mind for a couple of years, since I had seen a big eel attacking the gills of a freshly killed trout strung to keep fresh in the cold stream. On another occasion, three smaller eels were spotted behaving in the same way with two other trout, hung in the same spot. Each time it was the gills the eels attacked. Ken and I used gill portions on smallish hooks at the outset because we both felt that the eels would have to be struck rather quickly in the fast current. It was an entirely different situation from still-water eeling, where the fish could be allowed to run off with big baits.

Gerry, presumably after monsters, used bigger hooks and baits, but later changed over because of a number of indecisive pecks. Meanwhile Ken and I gave a demonstration of how not to catch eels. Bite after bite ended up with the eel in a solid mass of weed, and most times we were forced to pull for a break.

Not having had the good sense to study the swim and the weed beds by daylight, we had no idea how to steer the eels clear or bring them to the bank, and we found out eventually only by trial and error. The eels were not big. They were of a nice eating size, however, and just about big enough to lift out without a landing net.

We hung up a sack and dropped them into it as we caught them, tying on a fresh hook each time. I have never found out how to unhook a writhing, slippery eel in the dark, but as these fish were all going to end up as food for friends who like them, it mattered little.

Gerry finally got the bait size right, and I heard him whoop as his reel screeched in the darkness. He cranked and pumped away, bringing the eel upstream and, being by now completely accustomed to the darkness, I saw it coming across the top ready to be lifted out. But somehow it managed to dive into a great mass of weed near the bank, and for a time it was stalemate, with Gerry hauling and the eel wrapping more and more line around more and more weed.

I took the landing net and poked around until I could see the eel. It was jammed solid and there was no way of getting it into the net even if the wretched thing had not bent double when I poked.

Eventually I managed to part the weed with my hands and then, as the current swirled the eel surfacewards, I grabbed it by the throat, snapped the line and hurled it up the bank in one movement. Ken pounced on it, ready to do battle, but it had very little to say after that. At around 3lb it was the best eel of the night.

In all we landed eleven eels, but we lost at least double that number one way or another through our own fault. Not that it really mattered; it was basically a fun trip.

By around half past two in the morning we were all very tired, but because we had been so determined to fish all night, we had made no provision for sleeping. We had warm clothing, of course, we were wise on that issue, but the night was suddenly very cold when we decided to snatch a few hours' sleep and go trout fishing again in the morning. Fools that we were!

Gerry slept in the fishing hut, Ken and I in different cars because the concrete floor of the hut did not appeal to us. But I do not know which was the worse proposition.

I was cramped and cold, and my so-called reclining car seat made so many great ridges in my back that I longed for daylight to come. When it did, I could hardly move my stiff and aching joints, and I was met by two similarly afflicted individuals. It took two massive pots of tea to bring us back to life, during the drinking of which we were agreed that this kind of caper was for fools—or very young rugby players.

We did not trout fish any more, we were too interested in baths and beds to bother; but we took time out to skin and clean the eels before leaving. At least we were thought kindly of for that little gesture by the recipients; but I doubt if they'll ever know the sacrifices we made to provide them with their 'jellied and mash'!

Nostalgic Return

To you who have thrilled to the roar of rapids or relaxed to the whisper of a gentle stream, 'thank you', for it is a world we both can share. And in doing so, we become brothers.

Dan Gapen

In 1969 I travelled, with two American friends from Michigan, over the Mackinac Bridge and crossed into Canada by way of Sault Ste Marie or, as it is better known, 'The Soo'. From there, towing a boat, motor, gasoline, camping gear and a spare canoe, we headed north from Wawa and thence for 90 miles across gravel roads, pot-holes, ravines, washouts, log bridges, creeks, boulders, bogs and shale until we reached the lumber camp where we were to stay and fish. It was, I believe, two o'clock in the morning when we pulled alongside the home of Milton and Joan Vaillancourt, but they were awake and waiting for us with food and coffee. Milton, who had arranged for our permits, explained that there were 400 square miles of timber and lake country to be explored and that we could fish a different lake every day for a month if we so wished. Most were virtually unfished. Some of the lumbermen dabbled a little and caught walleyes for the pot but, in the main, these were utterly unexploited waters. All of which sounds like an angler's dream, but with so much water and so little time it is not easy to find a hot spot. We tried, however, and we enjoyed the trying!

When he could take time off from his responsibilities at the lumber camp, Milton joined us and told us all he had gleaned while working the territory. We had fun. We caught a *lot* of fish, mostly walleyes and pike, and we undoubtedly helped swell

69

the contents of Joan's freezer while we were there. As was only to be expected, of course, the big one we were looking for didn't show. But who was I to care? When you see, as I did, a moose, a bear, a beaver and a porcupine in the course of a single day, and you realize that you have never seen any of these creatures in the wild before, you tend to believe that there really *is* more to fishing than catching fish. The sight of a great bull moose, like some prehistoric monster, standing haunch-deep in the swamp, grubbing out lily roots, his great rack strewn with soft, stringy weed, was truly wondrous. The sight of a cow moose stepping unconcernedly into the creek a mere rod's length in front of the canoe we were paddling was frightening. Fortunately she merely swam to the far side and made a dignified exit into the bush. She *could* have turned us over had her mood been mean! These, though, are the experiences that call me back to wild country whenever the opportunity arises.

Where else could I sit and watch otters at play for an hour or more? Where else could I see chipmunks and other small squirrel-like creatures so tame? Or wild duck or loon or snipe or hawk that seemed not to object to human presence?

When I left I promised to keep in touch, and later I wrote a book that included a chapter on my experiences in the bush. It is not with me as I write, and so I cannot quote with accuracy, but I ended the chapter with a promise to return some day. It was a promise I truly meant to keep, and, eleven years later, I did so. It was not easy, and without the help and enthusiasm of my American friend, Tryg Lund, I could not have done so.

The town had grown, so too had the Vaillancourts' children. They had been so young in 1969 that they did not remember me; nor, in truth, did I them. The lumber camp had gone, the water was open to the public and, like so many other prolific waters of its kind, was rapidly being 'fished out'. Many waters having easy access and boat-launching facilities somehow or other appear to stop producing after a short term of exploitation. It has always puzzled me why vast waters such as these (waters that would be regarded as over-fished if they saw a dozen anglers in a week) should not hold incredible numbers of predatory fish. There is an abundance of food, and a myriad of minnows, perch and white fish exists there, yet the signs are that much of their vast area is devoid of takeable-sized fish.

Always, however, there is the hope of finding 'the lake that has not been fished', and I believed Milton when he said that there were waters nearby that had never had a line put in them. A large-scale timber map indicated that, if a certain small creek could be negotiated by canoe or boat upstream for a distance of several miles, such a lake would be revealed.

Looking at the first few yards of this overgrown creek—a mere yard wide in places—Tryg and I thought that such a trip might be possible and took the chance. On board we loaded the sixteen-horse-power motor, gasoline tank, tackle boxes, fishing rods, life jackets, food, waterproofs and, in the 90°F temperature, paddled towards our Shangri-La. Half-eaten by insects within the first few minutes, we began to meet obstructions. Overhangs and fallen trees we were able to cut away or squeeze under; beaver dams were another story. Unless you have ever tried to execute a portage over the swamp-ridden territory around a beaver dam, there is no way I can explain the difficulties involved.

It seemed that we were right. No living soul had ever navigated that creek or travelled the territory before. Or had they? Suddenly here was a rotting log bridge, obviously very old and now helping to support yet another beaver dam. That was the tough one. Lifting and dragging the loaded canoe over that obstacle, with rotting logs grinding to powder beneath our feet, was the most desperate task I have ever helped to undertake. Père Marquette himself could have faced nothing worse! But we made it and, after three hours, the lake opened up in front of us. At the far end an upturned boat was chained to a tree, and a polystyrene water bottle floated under the bushy bank! So much for Shangri-La.

We could find no other entrance, however, and, as I can state with complete confidence that neither *this* nor any other boat had navigated 'our' creek for many, many years, I can offer only two explanations: either the boat had been flown in on the wings of a light aircraft and dropped, or it had been brought in during the winter along an old frozen trail used by moose hunters. It had obviously not been used for a long time, and there was no evidence to suggest that the lake had been fished recently, if at all. It may not even have been a fishing boat; it could well have been placed there for duck hunting in the fall.

Tryg and I sat on the mossy bank where the boat had been inverted and chained to a tree. We wrote our names and a message on a piece of paper, wrapped it in foil and tucked it into the padlock. At some future date another sportsman would come along to use the boat he had struggled to launch in that wild and beautiful place, and we wondered what his feelings would be when he discovered that someone else had discovered *his* Shangri-La. He would ponder no doubt, as we had done, on the hows and whys of it all. But he would not worry. Our note told him that we had seen what we came to see and that we would not be back.

We took our bearings from that spot, and kept certain landmarks firmly fixed in our minds so that we would not lose track of the completely hidden exit back to the creek. The lake was huge; the shoreline looked virtually the same everywhere, and it would have been so easy to become lost. . . .

We worked the bays and reefs with plugs and spoons and caught pike. The sport was not fast and furious, but interesting. The fish were not large, mere five-pounders, but size is not important in such surroundings. Those few fish we caught fought like demons. They were lean and athletic, but not 'hungry'.

As the day wore on and the sun burned our backs, we sought the shady side of a big bay and bounced our plugs over the bottom rocks. A run-of-the-mill pike snatched at Tryg's spoon and tried to take off at speed. Suddenly a golden flash showed near the bows of the boat, there was an almighty swirl, and Tryg's very ordinary pike was seized by one of immense proportions. There it lay with a four- or five-pounder held crosswise in its jaws, refusing to budge, unaffected by the bucking of the little carbon fibre bait-caster.

As Tryg applied pressure, the fish stayed precisely where it was and the boat was drawn towards it!

It may have been the sight of the boat, or my shadow as I leaned forward with the gaff to try to 'chin' it out, but, whatever the reason, the big 'northern' took off at that precise moment.

There was never any doubt about the result, of course. The monster was not hooked but merely holding its prey. Tryg hung on hard at his end, and for a while there seemed to be a chance that he might coax it back into gaffing range again, but when it sounded beneath the boat in 12ft of water, we really knew that it was lost. After several minutes of stalemate, Tryg's plug came back with its treble hooks mangled beyond repair, and, with another flash of gold, the battle was done. (In the clear but peaty water of the lake all fish appeared to be gold in colour.)

We kept a five-pounder for a camp meal, and before the sun had sunk too low in the sky we made our return along that hazardous creek. The homeward journey was easier, since we had the current to assist us, but our portages were just as difficult. The beaver dams had been repaired in our absence, and the bogs and black flies were just as thick as before; but we made camp before sunset. Thoughts of spending a night in the swamp probably stirred us to greater efforts, and, as we hauled out the boat at the log trail bridge, Tryg summed it all up to perfection: 'I would not have missed it for a million dollars,' he said. 'But I wouldn't give a nickel to do it again.'

We ate the five-pounder that night as we sat around the camp fire, beginning to learn about muscles we never knew we had before.

And today, years later, when the heel I bruised on that trip begins to ache again, I am reminded of our trip to Shangri-La. I remember my bruised, grazed and aching body, the sticky-sweet smell of the fly dope, and my disgustingly filthy clothes. I remember my sodden boots and the black bog water I squeezed from my socks, and I remember that it was exactly three seconds from the time Tryg's head hit the pillow to the sound of his first snore. I do not remember hearing the second.

Mixed Blessings
From a September Diary

Peoria, Illinois. With an official estimate of 10.4 million acres of land under water in seven states, Jack Erhesman and I gave up the idea of trying to fish in any of the big impoundments here and chose instead to fish some of the local strip mines. It was a wise choice. Instead of thick soup we found crystal-clear water and luxurious weed growth. We also found some fish! True, they were not big fish, but at least they were eager biters, and our brief stay was enhanced by the fact that we were getting a fish every cast at one stage.

I've caught many largemouth bass up to 6lb during my several visits to this country, but I cannot recall a time when I caught so many in so short a period. I found it especially interesting, too, because, although it was strictly lure and jig fishing, we were able to fish the whole time from the bank.

When the water begins to warm up, largemouth bass start to work the shoreline for food, and it is the general practice, on big waters at any rate, to fish from a boat. The cast is made then so that the lure is placed an inch or two from the bank and retrieved through the deeper water towards the boat. It works well enough, and thousands of bass are caught that way each year. It's a method I've practised a lot in England too, for pike especially, and I've found it useful when the banks have been overgrown and the waterline difficult to reach from land. But I am sure that there are times when boat noises, particularly the rattling of oars on a wooden punt, do much to scare the fish away, and I believe that many fish here are also scared away by approaching boats, especially those with powerful engines. Leon Zedric, the fisheries manager on the Stripmines we visited, put forward an interesting theory, and one with which I agreed entirely. Bass, he said, often lie in wait several yards from the shoreline and drive their prey towards the banks where they can corner it in the shallow water, and a lure fished towards the bank instead of away from it probably appears more acceptable at certain times of the year.

Fun with a camera! Leon Zedrich poses behind a largemouth bass weighing
between 5lb and 6lb

We found it to be so. Nearly all the bass we caught were hooked close to the bank on which we stood, but there was strong evidence to suggest that our lures had been followed by fish lying out in the deeper water. I've no idea what the biggest fish we caught would have weighed, but I doubt if any went more than 12oz, and I've no idea how many we caught, as I stopped counting after we'd unhooked and released about fifty. But it was interesting and stimulating to say the least. We were using ultra-light rods, tiny jig-spinners and lines of about 3lb test. The little fish fought every inch of the way and often forced us to give line, so powerful were their outward runs against the tiny wands we were using. Later I changed to fly and had some real fun with these scrappy little fish. There would have been no enjoyment in it at all had we been using regular bass tackle but on our light outfits those fish were real fun to catch. I doubt very much if we could have handled any of the five-, six- and seven-pounders known to inhabit the lake we were fishing, but it would have been interesting to have had the opportunity!

No big fish came our way, however, but proof of their existence was there in the shape of three super bass that Leon had caught the day previously. They were alive and well in a large wire cage, and I admired and photographed them before Leon went to work on them with the big fillet knife.

'Stay to supper,' he invited. 'We'll have bass fillets and fresh picked mushrooms.' And he showed me a huge boxful of morels he had gathered that morning. They were sponge-like fungi, and although I have never eaten them, I imagine that Leon's proposed meal would have been a gourmet's delight. But I had a bus to catch that evening and I declined—reluctantly.

'Before you go,' said Leon, 'you must catch some of our red-eared sunfish. They're like bluegills and I know you'll enjoy them.' He knew, by now, that bluegills are my favourite American fish and he knew where they lay in abundance.

So, with our little jig rods, we followed Leon along the dusty trail (amazing after all that rain), coughing and spluttering in his wake. The sunfish were there, eager, scrappy little fish, weighing less than a pound but strong and beautiful, as their many-coloured bodies flashed brilliantly in the gin-clear water. How different this was from flogging away in the murk of the big lakes we had visited previously, and how good it was to see the shapes of fish swimming deep among the dark-green weed beds again. I would never have tired of it, I'm sure, but time was pressing and I reluctantly had to consider packing my rods away and getting back to the city.

Jack and I looked around for Leon, but he had disappeared and, in that vast expanse of land and water, there was no way we could find him. Nor was there any way for us to get out. Leon had locked the gates behind us and we were stranded. We were still stranded long after the bus I ought to have caught had left!

Then, over the brow of the hill came Leon. Rod in hand, hat pushed back, he staggered under the weight of a bulky haversack. As he came to a halt he remarked 'I thought you might like to take back a mixed bag, Fred, so I brung you some crappie!' And from the big haversack he tossed one, two, three, eight, fine black crappie. 'Now,' he said, 'get busy with your fillet knife.' I hadn't the heart to tell him I'd missed my bus, but in a way I was glad!

Later that evening at Jack's house, I teamed up with three fine young boys—fishermen in the making. Jack's son Doug, and Scott and Gary Matteson and I joined forces to catch bluegills from the small lake at the bottom of Jack's garden, while he worked over the outdoor stove frying smelt, crappie and bluegills for us to eat there and then.

Why is it, I wonder, that small fish cooked and eaten out of doors taste so good? They're delicious at any time but that fresh-air flavour has to be experienced to be appreciated. It's part of the American fishing scene, and I never tire of it.

I wish we in England had fish like largemouth bass and bluegills. I wish we had the climate to encourage us to do similar things. I wish we had vast waters to fish, and fish that were as easy for our youngsters to catch as those that are accepted naturally as part of the American way of life. I wish— but I could go on wishing. . . .

OCTOBER

In October I remember days with big rainbows and Indian summers and dace and the duckpond, and I begin to look ahead to pike fishing and, recalling one fish in particular, look forward to the winter.

F.J.T.

Sneaky

The trout season was almost over, and the banks of the little chalk stream were already showing signs of autumn gold. The weed had been cut some weeks previously and had never really made a comeback. The trout were spooky and, with few hidey-holes left, tore up and down the stream in panic at my approach. It was not a good fly-fishing situation, and yet the fish were there to be caught—if I was smart enough.

I had arrived at dawn after a long drive and, so cold was the morning, had spent the first two or three hours dressed in winter gear. Later, a weak sun threw my shadow across the water long before I reached its edge, giving warning of my approach to the already wary fish. It appeared hopeless, but I had a day to spend, and I do not give up easily.

I crossed the stream so that my shadow would not fall on the water and tucked myself under a big alder where I had last seen a trout dive off in nervous haste. I could see the clean gravel bottom through my polarizing glasses, and I studied the

78

dark water below the tangle of tree roots. There *ought* to be a fish there—even if I could not see it—and I waited for it to put in an appearance.

I had been there exactly an hour when a big rainbow cruised by, turned and went back upstream again. I froze. The fish began a regular patrol not obviously feeding but, I thought, possibly searching.

I put on a loaded shrimp pattern, waited my chance and flipped it in front of the fish as it came back yet again. It landed with a plop, and I could hardly believe my good fortune when I saw the trout change course and seize it before it had time to sink more than a foot.

For perhaps ten minutes I pressured, eased, teased and manoeuvred that trout into submission and, when I finally made to net it, it dived under the roots of the alder. As it did so another fish of equal proportions came out of the shadows. My net bagged in the current, but the fish was eventually enmeshed and lifted clear. It weighed 5lb 2oz—my best that season, and I was pleased. But there was more to come.

Two hours later, the second fish emerged from the alder roots, and I caught it in exactly the same fashion. It, too, weighed a fraction over 5lb, although it was a longer, slightly leaner fish. Even by today's giant standards that was still a pretty brace of fish. Not too demanding of casting skill, perhaps, but a fine example of what can be achieved by being stealthy, patient and downright sneaky.

Champagne and Sea Trout

Is there any better sight, I wonder, than that of a fresh-run salmon safely on the bank? That great bar of silver, with the sea lice still upon it, has a beauty of its own, and, although it has already provided thrills enough to its captor, there's still a great deal of pleasure to be gained from looking down upon it. A little pang of conscience, too, perhaps?

I catch far too few salmon these days, probably because I fish for them less often, but somehow I don't seem to care. To

FJT with a 9lb rainbow from the River Test

me there *is* a better sight than that of a fresh-run salmon: the sea trout is the fish that makes me tremble with anticipation before, and satisfaction after, its capture.

Does it sound phoney, I wonder, if I say that I would rather catch a 6lb sea trout than a salmon of twice that weight? It happens to be true. I have caught a fair number of ordinary rainbow trout weighing more than 6lb, and all of them have fought their hearts out, yet not one of them has given me the same satisfaction as a sea trout half that size.

Rainbows are not always easy to catch, but you can, by stealth, low cunning and a knowledge of their feeding habits, fool them into believing that your nymph or fly is good to eat. The sea trout doesn't often behave that way. In the little rocky rivers of the north, their grey shapes lie still in the clear pools and they are, in the main, uninterested in food. True, they will take food, but only if it comes within their immediate line of vision. Then they sometimes obey a natural instinct to take it, but I am sure this is a reflex action and not a real desire for food. You cannot study a sea trout and find out what it is feeding on before setting out to catch it. Things don't work out that way.

But you can, in the black of night, swing a great worm out into the gentle current and, by holding the line lightly on the forefinger, let it 'feel' its way across and down the pool where the sea trout lie.

You can pass them by a hundred times without the slightest reaction on their part, and, if you knew no better, you might be excused for thinking that they were uncatchable. You might, like many others before you, call it a night at one o'clock in the morning and make for the warmth of the cottage or hotel bed. Sea trout fishing can be frustrating to say the least.

But there comes a time, most nights, when the big worm stops in the middle of its gentle swing through the pool. A slight, but quite decisive, pull can be felt on the line as a sea trout mouths the bait.

This is the moment of truth, the critical stage when the novice may ruin everything by reacting violently and trying to set the hook. It takes nerve and a strong will to do *precisely nothing* at that point except poke the rod forward and allow the line to go slack. The sea trout may reject the worm completely, and it it does so you are back to square one. As often as not, however, the line will be felt to tighten slightly and pass through the fingers as the fish moves off with the bait. Then, barring accidents, the fish is yours. It is unlikely to shed the hook and the only chance of loss is line breakage.

There is, in my opinion, no finer fishing than this and no fish more richly deserved. By comparison the salmon is almost a non-starter in my book. . . .

There were about a dozen biggish sea trout in the pool and a great many more smaller ones. From the confines of a big alder tree on the high bank, brother Ken and I watched their blue-grey shapes in the deep, incredibly clear water below the shingle beach on the little Cumberland stream. They were restless in the low water and seemingly anxious to move upstream and go about their business of spawning.

A shadow thrown across the pool set them milling around in panic; a lure, fly or bait presented just then would be virtually useless. The very act of casting would do more harm then good, and so we watched and waited until nightfall. Such waiting can play havoc with a man's nerves. . . .

Hugh Falkus, the most skilful and knowledgeable sea trout angler I know, had told us not to be in a hurry. 'Wait,' he had said,' until you *think* it is dark enough, and then give it another half an hour before you start.' It was not the easiest of advice to follow, but it was sound, and we did just that. I am willing to swear, however, that both our watches went on a 'go slow' during those thirty minutes of waiting. Never have I known a longer period of frustration; but at last it was over, and we crept cautiously down to the water's edge and settled in for the night.

There was a long night of darkness ahead, and we had, perhaps, a mile of water that we could have fished had we so desired, but tonight we had been given a special privilege. Tonight we could fish the big pool quietly in the way we liked best to fish—with the worm and the light leger outfit.

The current above was lively, but it became almost nonexistent as it flowed into the pool. Seated on our stools, well back from the water's edge, rods held high so that the lines would not foul the bank, we fished almost as we would fish for bream and barbel in the Thames. But it was a more delicate form of fishing and much more difficult. The bottom of the pool was full of huge rocks, and the fish were lying deep, so we had to present our baits deeply, but without the use of lead for fear of snagging in the rocks. I have always regarded this as the most difficult form of fishing I have ever practised; it is easy to see why.

With a brisk current flowing, it is a simple matter to keep in touch with the bait. In an almost still, deep pool, it becomes incredibly difficult. Even without the use of lead, the tackle does not swing round and tighten naturally as it would in a more lively current, but it is still essential for everything to remain taut between the finger tip and the bait. Only that way can a bite be detected. To allow the bait to settle and rest on the bottom means snagging and/or eels. It also means that the line slackens and does not register bites if they come.

The only effective way of dealing with the situation is to cast well across the pool, allow the bait to sink and then *draw in line slowly* with the left hand so as to *feel* the bait bumping across the bottom. It takes only a couple of minutes to fish out each cast, and there is no question of putting the rod in the rest and waiting for a bite. If you do this the bait may become obscured and overlooked by the fish. Even if it settles in a smooth, clear patch, it is likely to be completely ignored by sea trout, which seem to prefer some movement in the bait.

Drawing in the line with the left hand, and holding it delicately between the fingers, gives a quiet awareness of what is going on below the water. The slightest pluck can be felt immediately, and that is important. Sometimes these sea trout take very gently indeed. The only drawback to this way of fishing is the amount of loose line that spreads around in the darkness as it is drawn in, but, as I see it, there is no real alternative. It could be argued, I suppose, that all you need to do is wind the reel handle slowly and retrieve line that way; but it doesn't work. I have tried it.

The first indication is likely to be a pull on the rod as a fish takes hold of the bait, and that will probably be the *only* indication received. The fish will spit out the bait and be gone before you can react. When a sea trout takes hold of a worm in the darkness, it is essential to give slack line immediately. You can not do this if you are cranking away at the reel handle!

That then, is how we fished through the long warm night. Hugh had warned us that any fish over 5lb was worthy of champagne, and that the captor would be expected to provide it next day. In the small spate river a fish of that size is a veritable giant, and, although ten-pounders are not unknown, they are too rare to contemplate. I had set my sights on something around the 5lb mark, and when I felt the first pull, I held my breath and wondered if this could be it.

I whispered to Ken that something had taken a hold, paid out slack line for a few seconds and then struck. The pool exploded, and a fish leapt clear of the water once, twice, three times, in a frantic dash downstream. The clutch screamed as I let it have its head, while trying at the same time to steer it clear of the overhanging branches on the far bank. I do not know how long it took to land; probably no more than about five minutes, but it seemed like an age in the darkness. At last Ken put the big net under it and lifted it ashore. A good fish, and I was pleased, but I felt sure that the fishing would be over now for the rest of the night. After that commotion nothing else could possible happen! Nor did it for about another hour and then, by a miracle, it was Ken's turn. His first ever sea trout by design; and I was pleased for him.

We carried them back in triumph over the dew-soaked meadows and went through the weighing ceremony. My fish was touching 6lb; Ken's an ounce under five. Our host rubbed his hands and beamed. 'Champagne, I'm afraid,' he said!

Did you ever eat a breakfast of immature sea trout, herling as they are called up there, cooked with crisp bacon and home-made bread? And champagne?

I confess I've never had champagne for breakfast before, but I hope it won't be the last time. I felt good afterwards, but I'm still not sure whether it was the champagne or the satisfaction of a good fish that gave me that inner glow!

My only regret is that Ken's fish didn't weigh an ounce heavier. Had it been so we would have had two bottles. Then perhaps I might have been more certain.

Rudd on Top

We were in the midst of what is usually referred to as an Indian summer. The owner of the lake had promised some large rudd to a lady for her big ornamental pond, and he asked me if I would be kind enough to go and catch some for him. Would I be kind enough indeed!

I knew this lake and the fish it held. Opportunity to fish such waters does not come often, and I had no intention of letting this one slip through my fingers. The rudd there grow big. They are brilliant gold with blood-red fins, and they are not too difficult to catch as long as they are treated with respect. From the bank the fishing is difficult because of overhanging trees and thick marginal rushes, so I chose not to fish at dawn but to wait until later in the day when I could use the boat.

I drifted towards the reed beds and anchored quietly. I threw a few loose crusts on to the surface and let them drift into the thicket while I put the rod together. A simple peacock quill float, cocked by one large shot, a No. 12 hook tied directly to 3lb line and baited with a lively brandling worm was all I needed in the way of tackle. The landing net was made up ready, and the large keep-net hung over the side of the boat.

Soon there were swirls around the floating crusts as the rudd began to attack them, and I dropped my float tackle as close to the reeds as I dared.

This is a remarkably effective way of catching rudd, but it calls for accurate casting. The single cocking shot is set near to the float so that the bait sinks slowly under its own weight. Rudd seem to prefer a bait that moves, and, almost invariably, the take comes before the tackle has straightened. The float glides away slowly *into* the reed bed, and for a moment the situation is a tricky one. If you strike too soon, the fish is not hooked; if you leave matters too long, you could lose both fish and tackle in that jungle of reed stems. Time things right, however, and you can briefly bully the fish into open water and play it out nearer the boat.

So it was on this day. I missed a number of fish through being what my friend Dick Walker would call 'too previous', but I lost no fish through breakage. By mid-afternoon I had caught more than enough, and I put aside eighteen fish averaging a pound apiece for the ornamental pond.

For the rest of the day I drifted around in the boat, casting here and there with pieces of crust on a completely leadless tackle, and I took some really good rudd right off the surface.

85

Some of them were over 2lb and the great swirls they made as they came up to suck in these soft, surface baits were very impressive.

It's good to catch fish by any method, but there's something just that little bit more exciting about taking them off the top!

If They Called That Work!

It is some time now since I took Paul and Les fishing on the Avon, but I remember the occasion very well because it was barbel time, and I had hopes of a big one. I remember, too, that I was puzzled about Paul and Les at the time. I showed them good chub swims, pointed out where we usually caught roach in winter, told them where I had seen barbel last and where I thought they might be now, and spent quite a long time outlining the general fishing.

Les pointed to a long glide of even depth below a wide corner, and asked about it. 'No good,' I said. 'It's full of dace. So is the next one round the bend.'

Since these two had been pestering me for an Avon trip for about two years, I thought that they would be interested in trying for some better quality fish and, having done my duty, left them to their own devices, each in what I considered to be a good chub hole. I wandered around doing some spotting for future reference, and it was probably two hours before I saw them again. They were fishing the two swims I had dismissed earlier, and with wide grins on their faces they were fairly hauling in dace. Their keep-nets appeared to be bulging with dace averaging between four and six ounces, and each cast brought a fresh one to net. They were efficient, I'll say that for them. Watching them feed, cast, trot, strike, lift out, unhook and start the sequence all over again was a study in time and motion. It was obvious that they had a mini-match going for them and that they were out to beat each other, but I could not for the life of me understand why anyone should want to travel 300 miles to catch dace.

I watched them for some time. Both were perspiring freely in the hot sun, both wanted to stop for a drink, a sandwich and a smoke, but neither of them dared to. I remembered again the profound statement regularly made by a dear old friend of mine many years ago whenever he saw me coming back from a day's rabbiting, plastered in mud, frozen stiff and collapsing under the load of ferrets, chads, nets and other trappings, or half dead with lack of sleep after a fishing trip.

'If they called that work, boy!' he would say, and I always understood. Not that it ever stopped me, of course, any more than it stopped this crazy pair from dace fishing when I repeated it to them.

But can you imagine it? Here was a glorious stretch of river, stiff with chub, trout and barbel, and they chose to fish for dace! There is no accounting for taste I suppose! I left them to it, of course. It was their day, but when they 'weighed in' about 40lb of dace each at the end of the day I honestly thought what a waste of time it had all been.

I am not very fond of dace fishing, and unless there is a problem, a different approach or a chance of some really big fish, I seldom bother with it at all. In fact, I become very cross when I am working on a roach swim and start picking up dace. Some anglers love them, however, and I have no doubt that I could learn a lot from them if I had a mind to. Dace experts, of course, have reached that stage of efficiency because they *love* what they're doing. Me? I get bored too quickly. I work hard until I get them going, but after I have caught a dozen or so all the same size and I feel deep down that the next fish and the next fifty fish are all going to be identical, I quit.

I have many times in the past 'worked up' an Ouse dace swim and got it going nicely before handing it over to a guest on the fishery. The dace of the upper Ouse do not interest me. As Joe Taylor once put it: 'They don't grow very big. You'd need to catch fifty before you got one half a pound and then it'd be a little chub!'

I have caught bags of 20lb or more from time to time, and I can remember catches of over 50lb that included a few roach and perch, but my main objective has been to *avoid* dace, and

I've usually set out to use baits that were unacceptable or too big for them to manage. Maggots and casters are the last on my list when I fish rivers holding a lot of dace, simply because I reckon that the business of catching and returning dace ruins my chances of catching better quality fish.

But, of course, I have often fished for dace exclusively and with regular dace tackle too when there has been precious little else to fish for. I have many fond memories of dace fishing, and there have been many October days when dace have prevented a blank.

Dick Walker and I once cut up a sheep and hung it up over two swims on the upper Ouse. We caught a lot of dace from those two swims because the maggots that dropped off the dead sheep attracted them from a long way off. But it did more than that. It established those two swims as dace swims for the rest of the season *and* helped us to catch chub from other places without having to deal with the small dace problem.

My good friend Billy Knott, an ex-London match angler who now lives in Cornwall, has a burning ambition to catch a 100lb of dace in one session, and I feel pretty confident he will do it. He has the spot staked out; it is just a question of timing. In autumn when that part of the river is in flood, there is a tremendous gathering of dace shoals into the one area, and Billy is confident that with an early start and a late finish (bearing in mind that the days are shorter) he can do it. He has been near his target on several occasions, and one of these days, who knows? But can you imagine it? Assuming those dace averaged 4oz, he would have to catch 400 of them! If they called that work!

On the other hand, I have certainly worked a lot harder for less than a dozen dace if I tell the truth. There is a time in October when the crane-flies are thick on the upper Ouse. They fly around and end up spent on the water surface, where they provide a tremendous harvest of food for the waiting dace. In one particular place, for a reason I do not pretend to understand, the dace are well above the average for the river. They weigh 10oz and really tear into those crane-flies. What I have to do, of course, is spend half the day chasing crane-flies for bait, half of the remainder recovering from the effort, and the rest of the time practising a very frustrating form of fishing.

Those dace *do* seem to know the difference between a naturally spent fly and one that's stuck on a hook. They also prefer the females, which are harder to impale. Every so often, however, I manage to dap one on the surface without it appearing too obviously phoney, and a dace comes up and whips it. Whips it is right too! I have never known fish so adept at sneaking a bait off the hook as these surface-feeding dace. They are past masters at it, and I would put my success rate at about one in seven. Those caught, however, are really lovely fish, and there is a great feeling of achievement on those rare occasions when the strike connects. I shall never catch a lot of dace that way, I know, but it is a form of dace fishing that I really enjoy. I sometimes catch a pounder, but then it's a little chub!

> *If you're too busy to go fishing, you're too busy.*
> Carl Ring
> *King of the Ozarks*

There is another form of dace fishing I enjoy too. It comes with fining flood conditions often, again, in October. The river is very fast, and the water is still high, but most of the colour has gone out of it. The big, wide, gravel bar, which is only a few inches deep in summer, is now under 2ft of water and racing like a weirpool. It might be possible to float fish it. A good match angler could probably dream up a way of doing so, but it is beyond my capabilities. The swim is only a few yards long anyway, and as float fishing would be a very frantic business, which would only present the bait for a few seconds at a time, I invariably leger in this spot.

Now it is possible that, by using a well-balanced swing or quiver tip, I could catch more fish, but that is not always the object of my fishing there. I like to accept a challenge and see just how many of these dace I can dot on regular tackle using the touch-legering technique. It is *not* easy.

I use small red worms sometimes, but mostly I use lob tails, which seem to produce more bites than any other bait in these conditions. The bites are unmistakable when they come. There is a pluck that I can really *feel* and that is usually accompanied by a sharp pull on the rod tip. These fish ought to be easy to hit, but they're not! The fast water keeps everything taut, and it is almost virtually impossible to give the fish time to take the bait properly. The bait is usually rejected immediately, and it requires an extremely quick reaction to set the hook.

They say that if you can hit one in three dace bites on leger you are doing well. I doubt if I have ever achieved anything like that rate of success, and I can recall times when one in thirty would have been nearer the mark! The more I have missed, the more frustrated I have become, and then the frustration has made me even more determined to beat the little perishers! I never really do, of course, but for some strange reason I stick at it even when I am sure I could get bigger and better fish elsewhere along the river. Conditions seldom last long enough to find the real answer, and by the following weekend the river is usually back to normal again. About once a year, however, I find myself with the same situation, the same problems and roughly the same results. I know I will never really master these dace, but still I keep trying.

Despite my professed dislike of general dace fishing, however, I have had some extremely pleasant sessions fishing for better-than-average fish on the Test. In October, with the water slightly up, I have found one or two places where the shoals move into comparatively slack water and hole up until the level drops.

Then I just sit and dangle for them. You could not really call it anything else. I simply set the float so that the bait trips along the bottom, put the rod in a rest and relax while the tackle goes round and round in the naturally slow-moving eddy. Occasionally I toss in a handful of maggots and watch them as they spread out and drift with the current. Most of those maggots stay in the eddy and keep moving round in a wide circle. I watch for them to reappear from time to time, and, as they almost invariably do so, I am sure that very few of them are washed out into the main stream. Every so often the float goes under, slowly and quite determinedly. I have learned that it does not pay to react too quickly because these dace have decided they're going to *eat* these maggots, so I pick up the rod and strike in a leisurely way.

I have caught bigger bags of fish by hard trotting in the regular dace swims, of course, but I've enjoyed the catching of them less.

I have had them up to 15oz from my special swims, and I always try to arrange my trips to suit their special conditions. Then I can fish for good quality dace without the bother of casting, controlling tackle or winding back. I can simply sit there until the fish come to me when they're ready. And no one could call that work.

Duckpond Success

They use to call it the Duckpond, but it was really a big back-water of the River Thame, and it was the scene of many desperate fishing escapades in the early days. Desperate because we knew so little of the ways of fish. Desperate because we had so little tackle. Desperate because there were so many of us on school holiday fighting to get to the best swims. We knew that those big bream were there because in the heat of the bright sun we could see them—lazily drifting across the top with their backs half out of the water. In those days it would have been impossible to throw a stone into the water without hitting one of those fish. But they never fed of course! We threw baits at them time and time again, but they just moved aside and let them sink past their noses.

I suppose we made a lot of noise and in doing so spoiled our chances of ever coming to grips with those fish during the day-time, and, on reflection, I realize that we ought to have fished for them at night, but in those days no one had even considered the possibility. Well you'd never see your float in the dark, would you?

91

We did, however, try for them during the early mornings. We were always able to get up at dawn and pedal our bikes to the waterside. It was part of our upbringing and indeed our very nature to be abroad early during the fishing season.

Sometimes I managed to sneak on ahead of the others so that I could get the best swim (or what was considered to be the best swim); sometimes I was beaten to it by an even earlier riser. It got to be a bit of a rat race there at times, this desperate struggle for the best swim. Not that it made the slightest difference really. Apart from a few roach and very immature perch, we never caught anything—best swim or not.

There was a blanket of surface weed over most of the water for a great part of the summer. The area where the bream showed was quite near to the bank, weed-free and in casting range, but there was another small hole right out in the middle that always looked interesting. No one could reach it of course. We had silk lines, wooden centre-pin reels and quill floats. The water was 8ft deep, and the hole wasn't much more than a couple of yards across, so, even if we could have reached it, we'd never have been able to put the tackle into it with any degree of accuracy. But this hole intrigued me. It had never been fished, and I figured that if I could just get a bait out there I might be in with a chance.

I had, at that time, an old 15ft pole in three 5ft sections. I used only the top two because I was hardly capable of wielding the three, but when I began to work out a plan for getting out to that hole, I decided that three joints would be better than two. So I strapped the reel on to the bottom joint with my super-exclusive reel fitting, which was made up of bicycle inner-tubing, and tied on another rod ring (made out of a big safety pin). Then I got to work on my porcupine quill float. First, I stuck a couple of medicine bottle corks on it and tied a loop of soft wire near the top so that it would slide up the line. (I wonder what my old friend, the late, great, Billy Lane would think of my early sliders.)

I made up my gut traces myself in those days. We all did. We had all our terminal tackles on wooden winders ready to tie to the reel line at the waterside. The trace I made up for my first attempt at long-range fishing was a real work of art in my eyes, but I shudder to think of it now! It was only 2ft long because I wanted the float to slide up the silk line and not be caught up in the knot that joined it to the trace. My weight was a piece of lead tubing taken from some electrical flex, and it, too, slid freely on the trace. My float-stop was a piece of bristle from a scrubbing brush tied to the silk line at what I considered to be the right depth. All of which was, I think, pretty smart for a kid in those days.

The lead, float and bait were all concentrated in the last 2ft of the tackle, and as such it was easy to cast. I tried the whole lot out over on the green before I went fishing next day, and I found I could swing it underhanded for twenty yards or more. I had to strip off the necessary line first, of course, and coil it at my feet before casting. Preparations completed!

It was cold. My friends had already started live-baiting for pike, but the bream were still in the Duckpond, and I wanted to try my luck before it got too cold. (We all knew that bream never fed in winter, of course, and time was running short. How things have altered since then!)

I climbed on to the brickwork of the old grotto 6ft above the water level just as dawn was breaking. I was alone on this cold Saturday morning and could have had the 'best swim' to myself, but I had made up my mind to fish that middle hole. It took three or four casts before the tackle dropped neatly in the middle and settled with the float, now up at its crude stop, lying at half cock.

I sat and waited in the quiet of the dawn, proud of what I had achieved and willing the float to go under. The resident otter paddled by with a big tench in its mouth, and I marvelled at its speed and silence. Suddenly and with no preliminaries, the float disappeared. I grabbed the rod and tried to strike, but the fish was already hooked. The big pole bucked in my hands and bent over at such an alarming angle that I all but went into the water. Then all went slack and I wound in a hookless tackle. Trembling now, I re-baited and cast again.

There was another bite, slower this time, and my frantic haste to strike was unnecessary. There was a slow thumping at the other end and I hung on, trying to get the fish to the surface. To let it have its head now would have meant certain loss in the dense weed, and my only chance was to try to skim it across the top. That is precisely what I did! The great bronze slab came flapping across the surface, as I wound it to a standstill and dragged it up the bank.

It was absolutely enormous! There never was such a fish caught from the Duckpond. It was by far the biggest fish I had ever seen on the bank. It looked as if it could be the biggest in the whole world.

Actually it weighed 3lb 8oz! No one really believed me. I didn't expect them to and I didn't care. I had had my moment of success, and my plans had worked!

The water was polluted shortly afterwards, and the fish were all killed. I never caught another bream from the Duckpond, and to this day I do not know if they are back or not. It was all very sad. I never saw the otter again either; and that was even sadder.

NOVEMBER

In November I look back to Australian beaches and black-boy trees, barbecues and midnight surf-casting and long-necked swamp tortoises and bushland and heat . . . and to chub and black slugs and to falling leaves and perch and fun with pike.

F.J.T.

The Wisdom of Youth

The weeds had partly died off and the bulrushes were jack-knifed with their brown tips trailing in the slow stream. It ought to have been perch-fishing time, but the perch in our little river had strangely disappeared. Those great shoals of fat, stripy pounders were no longer present. The morning was mild, a slight, misty fog had slowed me down and now hung in clouds over the river. In the old days it would have been drop in here, drop in there, worms, brandlings, in the stream, on the bottom, all combinations until a perch shoal was located. That was fun fishing and not too demanding on tackle, patience or technique, but today it had to be chub or dace. The river had little else to offer, and while the dace were nice enough fish, they were of no great size, and one tired of them after a time.

Better, in the circumstances, I thought, to do some creepy-crawly work for big chub. They at least were still there, as big and as difficult as ever they'd been, and I knew I'd be lucky if I

95

caught two all day. Chub can be very touchy about baits, and they're very easily scared. I spotted several in the still pockets, but they were not interested in anything I had to offer, and, after three biteless hours, I returned to the fishing hut to brew tea. I passed another chub on the way and marked it for later, but I didn't see it again. Some youngsters racing along the opposite bank scared it and, I'm sure, every other chub in the stretch as well. At first I was angry, but then I remembered my own impatient youth and envied them their enthusiasm. They wouldn't remember the river as I had known it in the past and, although they wouldn't catch fish, at least they'd enjoy trying.

I lingered over tea and sandwiches, watched a hare through the glasses, fed an aggressive robin some maggots and brooded over past times. Later, with nothing better to do, I wandered across to the wide, deep corner where the boys were seated in intense concentration over their rods. They'd made plenty of noise getting there, but now they were settled and fishing like veterans.

I saw a rod leap in one's hand, watched it curve over towards the water and heard the splash of a moderate fish skittering across the top. Dace it would be, of course. There were plenty in the deep pool, and with fine tackle they'd get them easily enough. But the fish that came out protestingly on the end of the groaning, short rod was no dace. It was deeper, and there was no silver sheen about it. A roach? No, not a roach either. I walked nearer, keeping out of sight as well as I could and watched the boy unhook a half-pound perch and slip it into the keep-net!

'Yes mister,' he said. 'We got seven so far *and* lost a big one. Last week we had fourteen. Caught 'em all on brandlings.' He lifted out the keep-net to show me the catch and assured me that he'd put them all back later.

'If you put 'em straight back you get no more bites,' he stated with authority.

He'll go a long way will that lad.

Cruisers

I do most of my chub stalking in summer and tend to fish selected swims in the winter. The two approaches are entirely different. In summer you creep and crawl, spot your fish and throw a bait to it in the hopes that it will land in the right spot and be taken immediately. In winter you have to weigh up the current and temperature and try to figure out where they are likely to be. Generally speaking, they will be lying deep in a comfortable current with some source of food near to hand and, by putting the bits together, you can usually locate them that way.

They seldom bask or feed near the surface in winter, but there are odd times when they will come up for floating crust baits. Very occasionally, on a bright sunny day, they will cruise near the surface for brief periods, and it would appear that, in these circumstances, their paths are fairly well defined. They may be seen to travel over a short stretch, back and forth repeatedly, with no obvious intent to do much else.

Summer fish tend to drift around in small pockets (where present); autumn and winter cruisers cover longer stretches of clear water, appearing first on the upstream journey and again, shortly afterwards, on the downstream trip. You will not spot them unless you *look* for them, however, and if that sounds obvious, let me explain that most anglers are usually too busy setting up their tackle and making themselves comfortable to spend time peering into the water.

Chub will not show in coloured or dirty water, but after a flood has cleared they will often start to move. Then, if you sit quietly, remembering that chub can see you in winter just as easily as they can in summer, you may spot one or more of these seemingly restless fish.

Obviously they are on the move for a reason, but I would not attempt to define it. They are not foraging, and it is highly unlikely that they will show interest in baits offered them while they are moving in either direction. I have no idea why this should be; I am simply describing my own experience.

At the downstream 'turn-around' point there is a chance, however, and many years ago I learned how to induce a November cruiser to take. I baited with a piece of crust about half the size of a match box, pinched a swan shot immediately above it, and let the float take it downstream.

When it reached the 'turn-around' point, I held the float back in the stream so that the bait rose quickly in the water. There was a swirl near the surface, the float disappeared and the rod was nearly snatched from my hand. I had watched my chub, judged it to be at its downstream limit and tried to make the bait rise attractively in its line of vision. That particular chub was just under 5lb—the best from that water for some time. I have had more since by employing the same tactics, but none has been bigger than that first cruiser. I learned over the years, however, that it does not always pay to pick an attractive swim and go to work on it. Some of the fish I have taken by the tactics just described came from spots that I would normally have passed by without a second look.

In Lighter Vein

I had in mind to use some special little weighted flies Ken ties for perch when Frank Guttfield, Dick Barder, Ken and I went to a lake in Berkshire, which we knew had held perch in days past. It turned out to be one of those days. It usually does, of course, when Dick Barder is involved! He has only one thought in his head and that is catching pike. Apart from trout, he just does not recognize the existence of other fish. Perhaps that is not quite true, because I remember he really is keen on tench, and it was a letter on a tench-fishing problem that brought us together in the first place. But from September onwards he can think only of pike, and I suppose he was still thinking of pike when he drove past the lake where we were due to meet.

We had arranged previously to meet at 9.45, but he had said, 'Give me a few minutes either way—won't you?'

Either way? 'That means he'll be *late*,' I told Ken and Frank. He was. All this talk of missing the entrance and driving past didn't fool me! He was the member, I was his guest, and it can be embarrassing when the bailiff turns up and asks for your authority to fish. Ken and Frank had no problems. Their tickets were in order; by rights, however, I ought not to have been fishing at all.

There was much upheaval and a million excuses when he finally arrived and proceeded to unload his gear. Dick Barder is the only man I know who carries his tackle in eighteen small parcels instead of, like the rest of us, eight or nine big ones. On the other hand, he is well organized really. He can stuff those eighteen parcels into various pockets and no one could tell he was going fishing at all but for his rods.

While Ken and I chose to fish for perch, Frank and Dick put out dead-baits for pike, and, as is always the case when friends meet up after a long time, the social side got the better of the fishing side. That is part of what fishing is all about anyway, and leg-pulling is important. It helps do away with the idea that fishing has to be deadly serious, and on an occasion like this the catching of fish was just incidental.

Perch—from the good old days!

I left my weighted fly hanging in the water below the rod point while I talked, and then decided that if I was going to talk I might as well let the tackle fish by itself. I stuck a worm on the fly and let it dangle.

We stood around the tackle, all fishing close together, and Dick Barder kept muttering about the lack of sun. 'Why must you keep nattering on about the sun?' Ken asked. 'It won't show today old son.' Dick looked him straight in the eye and said 'Dammit—I want to know the moment the flaming thing's over the yard arm, don't I?' I groaned. I had been fishing with Dick Barder before.

He was producing four glasses and a bottle when my rod tip went into the water, and I struck into what I hoped would be a perch. The line parted near the hook, however, and, as I had felt a big fish briefly, I could only assume that a pike was responsible. Strange that. Three lots of dead-bait tackle and on the bottom, and a pike took a lobworm suspended below the surface.

I caught a pike on one of the weighted flies later, and Ken caught a perch around the pound mark. We all, I believe, caught little pike on dead-baits during the morning—which helped pass the time.

The staging where we fished was wet and greasy; there were also a number of boards missing, which made the going treacherous. The rain fell continuously—not heavy, but enough to make fishing a little uncomfortable—and so we took a few steps back and talked in the shelter of the trees.

'Wouldn't it be great,' said Dick, 'if we could just fish like this all the time and *still* catch something decent?'

'We will,' I said. 'We will. Just don't be in too much of a hurry, that's all.'

Dick went to look at his rod. With a sandwich in one hand, glass in the other, he ventured across the wet boards, slipped through a gap and fell with an almighty crunch. Sandwich went one way, glass went the other. I rushed to pick him up—then thought better of it: he weighs more than I do.

'It's all right old chap,' he gurgled. 'The glass was empty!'

About then Frank's line began to twitch, and he made his way gingerly out on to the narrow remains of an older staging, most of which was either rotten or missing, to pick up his rod. I don't know what sort of bite he had but I saw him hit a pike at fair range and start cranking it in. 'It's only a little one,' he called, 'but I may need a net.'

The pike surfaced and looked to me to be 20lb or so. 'You'll need a gaff,' I told him. And I stood by.

Frank and I are good friends, but we disagree about gaffs. Barbaric he calls them. This time, however, he needed me to help land his fish, and I was about to show him how to do it cleanly and with no fuss, using a gaff under the chin. He couldn't argue.

'Play it out and bring it alongside,' I instructed.

'But what if it goes through this blanking stage,' he wailed.

'It won't,' I said. 'Not if you play it out first.'

It did! Not only did it go through the staging, it went under about three of the inverted U-shaped arches that supported it too.

I did not want to see the fish lost but, since I could do nothing to help, I just laughed. That did not help at all! Frank had the job organized very quickly, however. He passed the rod under the staging and through the arches one at a time until the tackle was clear again. Then he took charge.

'This time Taylor,' he yelled, 'we'll have the flaming net.'

And not wishing to see poor old Frank suffer any more, I obliged. It was a bit of a squeeze, but I got it in first time and heaved it ashore.

It *looked* like a twenty-pounder and it *felt* like one too when I lifted it, but in fact it weighed just over 18lb. A very good fish, despite Frank's obvious disappointment, and one that fought extraordinarily well. He said at the time that he had caught bigger fish with a lot less spirit, and I went along with him on that. A good double-figure fish often fights a lot harder than one weighing more than 20lb, and that is what made this one all the more disappointing.

There was just the mildest hint of apprehension on Frank's

part when the fish took off under the stage (*panic* would be a better word), and we pulled his leg about it afterwards. But although we would never have admitted it at the time, the way he got himself out of trouble (which I had probably landed him in anyway) was a masterpiece of quick thinking. He deserved a twenty-pounder for that little episode alone.

Grayling Failure

It was, perhaps, too early to go fishing for grayling with serious intent, but at the end of the trout season, with thoughts of snowy fillets in lemon sauce, I went nevertheless.

I had located, and failed to catch, a small shoal of these interesting and generally obliging fish during the summer months. They would have none of my trout flies at that time, but, now I was allowed to use bait, I felt I might fare better. I might also be able to combine my grayling venture with a spell of roach and dace fishing for, in this little Hampshire stream, all three species often hole up together.

My grayling hot spot, however, failed to produce. I could see every inch of its fine gravel bed, and there was not a fish in sight. I walked the stream and spotted an odd fish here and there, but nowhere could I find sign of even a small shoal. The fish that were laying there so thickly in summer were now strangely gone.

An eruption in the vicinity of the overhanging elder bush told me why. A marauding pike had taken up residence in that rich feeding area and had obviously split up the shoals. I watched and presently saw its spade-like tail sticking out from below the streamer weed. I could not see its head, but by the same token I figured it could not see me either.

It was not a big pike, but it was too big for the comfort of this small stream.

I had no pike bait, but I had a feathered jig, which resembles a small fish, and I dropped it in by the pike's tail with a plop, again and again and yet again. I have successfully practised this little piece of subterfuge before and it worked again today.

Without bothering to look at the cause of the plops, the pike swirled and seized the jig.

For a time bedlam reigned but, in due course, I slipped the net under it. It weighed a fraction under 5lb and, though tiny by pike standards, was fun to catch on a light bait rod.

That it will upset no more grayling shoals is now absolutely guaranteed. It was transformed into 'pike au gratin' the same evening and served as an excellent substitute for the anticipated grayling in lemon sauce.

Winter Plugs

No matter how sophisticated an angler you may be, fishing will always have an element of mystery. If the mystery and the challenge weren't there, fishing would not be a sport.

Mark Sosin

'It's a waste of time fishing for pike with plugs after October,' said a friend who lives on the Norfolk Broads, and a few years ago I might have been tempted to agree with him. But not today. I have been interested in plugs for a long, long time, and, while I believe they are likely to be less effective in the dead of winter, I know that they can still be used all season to good effect.

I am convinced that there is a plug to suit almost every pike-fishing situation, though I would be the first to admit that it is not always easy to find it, and I agree that the average angler is not likely to be able to carry enough to deal with all eventualities. Nevertheless, modern plugs have their uses even in the coldest of conditions, and the actions of some of the latest models have to be seen to be appreciated. Perhaps 'seen' is not the right word. 'Felt' might be more appropriate, for you can feel the action of a modern, deep-running plug throbbing through the rod tip even though it is too deep to be visible.

Deep-diving plugs have been available for many years, and I have always preferred these to the ones that have to be helped down by lead weights. The addition of an uptrace lead will have some effect on the action of any plug, and that effect is almost invariably for the worse. Sometimes the action is completely ruined, for the truth of the matter is that good plugs are mostly designed for use without leads. Floaters and shallow divers are made to perform those two functions: to float or to dive a few feet only below the surface. Cramming lead on the trace will take them down deeper, but they are not intended to fish this way. And, generally speaking, these last-mentioned are not very good winter lures, although they are fine when the water is warmer, and the pike more inclined to feed near the surface.

It is unwise to generalize about anything to do with fishing, however, and pike, being the cussed creatures they are, will break all the rules anyway, but in my opinion, slow-moving deep divers are a good bet at this time of year.

The latest range of deep-diving American plugs comes in a great variety of shapes, sizes and colours. Of them all, I am most impressed with those having an ultra-modern metallic finish. This finish, still in a great many colours, shows up well at depths of up to 15ft, and I see it as the possible answer to some of our coloured water problems.

These extra-flashy lures will not be of any great value in clear, shallow water, but they show up well in conditions of fining flood.

Because they float at rest but dive deeply when retrieved, they are much easier to control than spoons. Their buoyancy allows them to be worked slowly, and on a really cold day that is the best medicine I know for a big and lazy pike. And big pike usually are lazy—or at least they appear to be so until they're hooked. For some reason, best known to the pike, the action that follows when a pike is hooked on a plug usually outshines anything that occurs during live- or dead-baiting operations. It is better and livelier during a mild spell, of course, but even in cold conditions pike will take off and clear the water when light and limber rods are used.

Light, limber rods make pike fishing fun, and their suppleness does not prevent the use of lines of reasonable strength.

Somehow we seem to regard ultra-light rods as demanding of gossamer lines in this country, but it is not necessarily so. The fun comes from using a soft rod, but the insurance against loss lies in the use of a substantial line. And when a pike, lying deep, hits a slow-running plug, the sensation at the rod end is incredible. There is nothing quite like it. Oddly enough, small pike give the most savage of wrenches; extra large fish often take quite gently and show their strength on the surface later. And if you're using a rod with some real bend in it you can take chances and enjoy some exciting action without losing the fish.

Plug fishing with little 'stick' rods is piking at its best. It's not always 'on' of course. The best days are those when the smaller fish are on the prowl. You don't go looking for big pike with that kind of outfit although the chances are always present.

There is a general feeling among many pike anglers that the days when no pike seem to be moving at all are likely to be the days when the really big one takes hold. Days when pike can be seen actively slashing near the surface, chasing fry and following lures with abandon are likely to be those that produce only small pike. It isn't always so, but it is generally a fair indication. Would those small pike be on such a rampage if the really big fellows were on feed too? One of the most satisfying meals for a big pike is another, smaller pike. Those fellows aren't particular!

I could relate a number of instances when this applied, and I am reminded that my two biggest-ever pike were solitary fish. I recall one memorable example of this particular pike lore. Spread over two lakes in Buckinghamshire, one very cold morning, were several anglers. By mid-day they were very despondent pike anglers, and I was one of them.

The east wind didn't help matters, and I believe we were all of the same mind really: we were wasting our time. But, as always, someone tried to keep our flagging spirits up by quoting that old 'this-is-the-day-we-might-get-a-big-one' bromide. We'd heard it all before of course, and, generally speaking, we believed it, but not today. Today they really were 'off'.

At least they were until the junior member of the party came dashing up demanding 'scales that will weigh up to thirty pounds'.

'I got me a biggie,' he bubbled. 'On a plug in the deep channel—must be over twenty pounds.'

In fact it weighed 18lb 8oz, but it was a superb fish and one we were all pleased to see. It didn't matter then that the only other fish of the day was a mere pounder taken from the margins.

Once again the old lore had been proved right and a plug had been found to suit the day in question.

The fact that the big fish came from the deeps and the small one from the shallows helped bear out yet another theory put forward in recent years. It is believed that small pike will take refuge in the weedy margins when strong winds cause a disturbance and move the big ones out. It seems to be a fact that pike will not stay put in the margins in these conditions. It could be that their natural food is forced out or that these big fish just become irritated by the continual movement of the rush stems. Whatever the reason, there seems to be no doubt that they prefer the open water when high winds are blowing—a fact which may be worth considering during those seasons when March 'comes in like a lion'.

West Australia

From a November Diary

The first soft rays of dawn are filtering through the patio screens and making shimmering patterns on the opposite wall.

A trail of silver-sand footprints, swimming trunks slowly drying and stiffening next to my skin, and a white powdering of salt on the hairs of my legs, serve to remind me of the night just past.

Had anyone told me I would spend a November night bare footed and ankle deep in soft sand, casting into the surf, I would probably have curled up with laughter. But that is how last night was. Traditional beach-casting attire out here consists of shorts, bare feet and tee-shirt (optional). It's quite disconcerting

FJT in the Australian bush—and a blackboy tree

to leave home in the afternoon wearing next to nothing and to know that the dark hours are going to be spent without the added warmth of extra clothing.

Having suffered the torments of a winter's night on Dungeness years ago, and having also felt my whole body freeze slowly like the cod adhering to Walton pier, I long ago decided I was not cut out for sea fishing at night. I have spent many sunny summer days by tench and carp lakes in the United Kingdom knowing full well that when the chill winds of the night arrived I would need winter clothing to see me through till morning. It has always been second nature to me to take especially warm oversuits for any kind of night fishing. Here, when the air cools and makes its presence known, you simply wade into the warm surf to take away the chill!

Bait-boxes, tackle, food and drink are centralized around traditional pressure lamps as they are around most English beaches. Tripods and rod holders are conveniently situated for baiting up, but, generally speaking, rods are hand held to feel for bites. It is all new to me. Casting with a multiplier and a long beach-caster never was my speciality. With a short, crank-handled rod, I am reasonably accurate, but long-range fishing with the heavier gear comes hard. In the darkness it is especially difficult; I prefer to use a big fixed-spool reel and accept the slightly reduced distance.

On a good night it seems that distance is not of too great importance, but, like everywhere else in the world, good nights are the exception rather than the rule. Extra casting distance seemingly increases the odds in your favour. The reef, about a quarter of a mile out, takes the brunt of the sea, breaks up the big waves and makes the beach water fishable. By day, they say, the fish are on the far side of the reef; by night they venture over it.

It would seem to be so. I had great difficulty in differentiating between pulls from loose seaweed and bites from fish *until* I had my first real bite. Then there was no mistaking it, and yet I could not tell you *why* I knew that this was the real thing. It's a kind of instinct, I suppose, and is exactly the kind of certainty that comes to the experienced leger-fisherman. Out of a hundred 'weed bites' in the river, he can pick out and strike at the one that comes from a fish. He cannot tell you *how* he knows, but he does.

There was no indication of the size of the fish I hooked, but, after a few moments, I began to realize that it was not something to be cranked in quickly. I lost control of it for most of the time because I was not familiar with my tackle, but I gained a little line every so often. In the end, however, it beat me. It set off strongly and, helped, I'm sure, by a great ball of loose weed, finally broke off over a hundred yards out. That little episode left me trembling. It is a long time since I felt such power, and I still have no idea what the fish was or how big. Roger and Ian, my two companions, asked all kinds of questions to try to figure out the species. Had either of these two hooked it, it's possible that they would have had some idea. To me it was just me hanging on at one end and something pulling like the devil on the other!

Roger cranked in a small 'pike'. 'It wasn't one of those at any rate,' he assured me.

I have to be honest, I don't know the true name of the fish referred to as 'sea pike' but, at first glance, they look extremely like our own esox. They're not, of course, and I suppose it's possible that they're related to the barracuda. I've only ever seen one barracuda (one that beat itself to death on the bottom boards of a boat in the Red Sea while I was slowly dying of sea sickness!) so I am hardly qualified to comment.

We all had our chances last night, and Ian came nearest to real success. He fought a stingray for at least twenty minutes before getting it to within gaffing distance. He warned me to stay clear and let Roger do the necessary. A swipe with the tail end of a 30lb 'stingie', they say, is *not* funny! I believe them!

'It's now or never,' said Ian. 'I can't fight it any longer.' And he clamped down on the reel, walking back up the beach as he spoke.

A wave swept the fish (it looked enormous) on to the sand, Roger plunged with the gaff, missed, and the returning wave swept the fish back into the water. There was a sound like a rifle shot as the line parted, and Ian collapsed in a trembling heap on the sand. For a time he could not speak, and I just *know* he'll never forgive Roger for missing. Ian has caught skate well in excess of 100lb, so it says much for the power of the 'stingie' if it can so demoralize such a man!

It is traditional, I suppose, in such circumstances, to pour out a cup of hot coffee or tea from the flask and take a break. We sat down and solemnly pulled the tags off three cans of ice-cold beer and drank our fill.

The weed was increasing, we were all tired, but we had enjoyed our exciting moments. Another night some other fish may decide to come inside the reef. There may be fewer problems and, as the season progresses, the nights will become warmer still. There is a lot to be considered and the opportunities are great.

Pike on a Fly Rod

Pike will take lobworms at times, but I do not recommend lobworms as standard bait, any more than plummets, paste or potatoes, which pike will also take occasionally. Orthodox baits give us quite enough scope . . .

H. T. Sheringham

My beginnings were, of course, centred around coarse fish and the ways and means of catching them because, at that time, there was no game fishing available to me. Things are different now, and, while I do not profess to be anything more than a very poor fly caster, I do regard myself as a fly fisher. There *is* a difference. It is hard to define but, like many other converted coarse fishers, I have learned to apply basic watercraft to the catching of trout, and my coarse-fishing experience has helped enormously in this respect. I also find myself extending my fly-fishing 'season' for as long as possible.

My experiences have also changed my general attitude somewhat, because I now find myself interested in applying game-fishing techniques to the capture of coarse fish. I am becoming

A modest pike caught on a lure

more and more convinced that coarse-fish anglers should become hunters of fish rather than technical perfectionists, and that we would do coarse fishing a service if we followed the game fishers' example and removed some of the fish we catch. Most of our waters are already overstocked, and I see no earthly reason why I should not take away the occasional fish for the table. I will always maintain my right to do so. Pike and perch are obviously the two most palatable species, but where perch stocks remain as low as they are in some waters, I would hesitate to recommend their removal for the table. Pike are different, however, and although they can be difficult to catch at times, there is a superabundance in many waters.

The trouble is that we set our sights too high. We think in terms of twenty-pounders, and tend to regard smaller pike as nuisance fish. But they need not be. They can provide good sport (and good eating) if caught on the right gear, and for sheer fun and excitement fly tackle is ideal.

There's very little enjoyment, in my opinion, to be obtained from catching a 6lb pike on a heavy-duty rod, wire trace and a live-bait; but take that same fish on a fly rod and it is a different story. I would, in all honesty, prefer to catch an eight-pounder that way than a twenty-pounder on traditional pike gear. And with a mounted twenty-eight-pounder and a thirty-two-pounder glaring down at me from the wall of my study as I write, I feel I can say that without being subjected to knowing winks and nods!

I think that fly fishing for pike opens up a whole new field and offers a superb opportunity for fly fishers to extend their limited season well into November, or even later, depending upon conditions. And I venture to say that, pound for pound, a pike will pull just as hard and for just as long as any trout. Unlike many of my fly-fishing friends, whenever I catch an accidental pike, I do not throw my rod on the ground and my hands in the air in a fit of histrionics. Nor do I kick the pike up the bank to rot. I am usually delighted because I already have a freezer full of trout but very few other white-fleshed fish. I take it home, fillet it, and either eat it there and then or freeze it for eating in due course.

Most Novembers I take my fly rod and fish exclusively for pike on flies I have dreamed up for that specific purpose.

I will not try to convince anyone that fly fishing is the dead-liest way of catching pike. It is probably the least efficient of all methods, but it *is* by far and away the most exciting and rewarding. Those who love to fly fish and who are not interested in other methods should try it. They will, I promise, become as firmly hooked as the fish they catch. It really takes hold. It has been said that pike are in poor condition in summer and that it takes hard frosts and prolonged cold spells to put them into top gear, but this is positively not true.

Pike, having spawned early enough to enjoy a bonanza period of feeding on the more vulnerable later-spawners, are in fact the first to recover. They are in excellent fighting shape from June onwards and because, for some unexplained reason, their peak feeding period seems to occur in November, they

The special glove and hook-removing tool shown here ensure that the handling of this pike does it no harm and allows it to be returned alive to the water

offer a real chance for fly-rod sport at the tail end of the trout season.

There are problems, of course. Pike can very easily bite or saw through a fine trout leader, and it is virtually impossible to incorporate a wire leader successfully on a fly outfit. But it is possible to compromise, by tying in a short, 6in tippet of 20lb test line at the end of the fly leader. Alternatively (and I have found this to be a very useful dodge), the tapered leader can be reversed so that the thick end is nearest the fly. There must be some kind of compromise here, too, of course. There's not much real sense in reversing a complete 9ft tapered leader so that it is joined to the fly line with a 2lb point! That is asking for trouble. But, while I make no claims at expertise, I have found that a 6ft leader is adequate and more easily controlled than a longer one. I shorten my leaders by cutting off the thin section before making the join.

I cannot cast big pike flies long distances but I have found, generally speaking, that I do not have to.

I use what is commonly referred to in the United States as a bass-bug or saltwater-taper fly line, and do as little false casting as possible. These fly lines are designed to be picked up and turned over just the once. It is a case of pick up, back cast and shoot. No rod waving, line extending or unnecessary swishing back and forth. The object is *not* to achieve distance but to get back fishing as quickly as possible.

Some experiment may be found necessary with the regular fly lines obtainable here, but it is possible to achieve the same result by cutting an old, double-taper fly line to the right length and splicing it to a length of dressed shooting line. Monofilament backing is, in my opinion, not suitable for this work.

Almost any big streamer fly will catch pike, but it is fun to experiment with monstrous creations of your own design and to try different depths and retrieval rates until the right one is found. When water is highly coloured, chances are greatly reduced, and the same applies when the margins are fringed with ice. But that is one of the nicer aspects of fly fishing for pike. It can be practised in comfort.

DECEMBER

In December I recall days with chub and Wotton and iced margins and Christmas in the cold of England . . . and the heat of Western Australia . . . and skippies and beach-combing for shells . . . and silver sand and lost kingfish.

F.J.T.

A Sporting Christmas Day

Christmas to us, ever since we were kids, was the time when we needed pike baits because we always went pike fishing on Boxing Day. In the early years we had to keep the baits alive because we believed, quite wrongly, that only live-baits would catch pike. Today, of course, we can use artificials and sprats and herrings from the fishmonger's, and in any event there is always a goodly supply of dead roach, dace and rudd baits in the freezers, so we're never short of Boxing Day baits. Somehow, however, it doesn't seem quite as exciting as it did then. Our fishing was hard, our winters seemed to be hard too, and our tackle was crude by today's standards. Pike rods were really only roach rods with shorter, stiffer tops, and the old wooden reels didn't make casting easy, but we caught pike on them.

I suppose there *were* Boxing Days when we failed to catch pike, but I don't remember them. I remember the local canal, its banks hard with frost, and the local characters who always

115

Hugh Gough and FJT with a netful of pike-baits

used to fish for pike on that particular day. I suppose we were pests in those days, but it was there that we learned the horrors of gorge-baiting (now outlawed of course) and of pike-bungs and snap-tackles. It was there that we kids earned extra coppers by catching live-baits in advance for the adults who couldn't afford the time to catch them for themselves. That, or they weren't quite as smart as we were when it came to tapping quick-biting canal roach on hempseed! Whatever the reason, they were always glad to buy them from us for the traditional Boxing Day bonanza. I think they really *did* go fishing to catch fish, but the little groups that gathered around the various bottles and baskets of goodies, helped show that this was a social event as much as a fishing trip.

I didn't have any gorge-tackle in those days, nor did I have any snap-tackle or a pike-bung, but I managed with an eel hook, some thick gut and a big cork. I'd sell my little roach baits, but I'd hang on to the gudgeon because they were livelier and, being smaller than the roach, better suited to my improvised gear. I realize now, of course, that to some extent I was fishing better than most of the grown-ups. My lighter gear, unencumbered by big leads, hawsers and pilot floats, allowed my baits freer movement. I never caught any big pike—but then no one else did either!

I missed those trips for five years while I was in the Middle East, and when Christmas came round each year I thought and wondered if the same old gang would be fishing the canal or the pits or the lake on the big estate as they'd done so often in the past.

When I came back to England I dug out as much of my old tackle as I could and took it back to camp with me because, up in the Fylde district of Lancashire, there were some pits and canals, and I'd met another soldier who was just as enthusiastic as I was when it came to fishing and other field activities. Tommy was a fitter, and much of the tackle we needed was fashioned in the unit workshop in Lancaster. We loved the outdoors and, being servicemen, tended to forget that we were poaching waters controlled by clubs or syndicates and even

117

owned privately by men of wealth.

I poached my first two salmon up in that area, and Tommy and I shot wild duck and rabbits on the estate where we were stationed. I 'acquired' a 14lb tin of treacle and swopped it for a ghastly single-barrelled twelve-bore shot gun, and Tommy and I loaded our own cartridges with black powder and mixed shot. We bought a ferret, too, and that year our winter was complete.

The Unit had a regimental party on Christmas Day 1944; but this highlight of the serviceman's year was carefully avoided by Tommy and me. We hid ourselves in the garden shed until the detachment had driven off to join the main unit for breakfast and then made a dive for our gear. This may have been Christmas Day and a time for celebration, but it was also a day for doing the things we really wanted to do, and Tommy and I had plans.

We had a can of pike baits, some maggots, some re-load cartridges and Ferdy the ferret all ready to go. The canal was a long mile across country from where we were billetted, and we'd seen a pike strike on a wide corner there several times

Ken Sutton inspecting a catch of pike

previously. That was the real purpose of our party-dodging, but, because we had to walk across good game country to reach it, and because there were rabbit burrows along the canal bank, we went prepared for any eventuality!

We used up all our baits, but we finally caught the pike. It was a seven-pounder and it took at about mid-day. It was a good fish for that stretch of water, and we strung it up to bear back in triumph for a local civilian who had expressed a liking for pike cutlets. We'd caught, if I remember rightly, four nice roach and a small perch before we caught the pike, and, when bites had ceased, we let the pike outfit fish by itself while we ferreted along the bank.

We killed three rabbits including a black one (common enough in those days), and with those, a pike, an empty bait can and our rods slung about us with various pieces of string, we walked back across the kale field and shot two cock pheasants!

I've fished before on Christmas Day and I've either shot or ferreted on Boxing Day, but I've never practised all three kinds of sport before or since on the same day of the year. Free time was short in those days, and it wasn't often that such chances came our way. Our 'mixed bag' was the result of our making the most of a golden opportunity.

It was dark when we arrived back in camp and the detachment was back from main barracks. Some of them looked decisively the worse for wear, some were still a little merry, but all, without exception, raved about the good time they had enjoyed and what fools Tommy and I had been to miss it. We did nothing to enlighten them. Tommy winked and agreed that perhaps we had made a mistake, and I said yes, it must have been a grand occasion. Little they knew!

Lunch or Laundry?

When the war was over and life back to near normal, pike fishing again became our traditional Boxing Day sport. We were fishing at Wotton Lakes in those days, and our big con-

119

verted pontoon boats were ideal for cold weather piking. We had folding canopies to keep off the wind and a big oil stove aboard to brew tea and keep us warm.

Joe Taylor, who fished with brother Ken and me in those days, was a bit late starting on Boxing Day 1952, but he made the boat on time after grabbing a carrier-bag of food for the day from the kitchen table. Darky, a member who regularly pike fished from a similar pontoon, arrived about the same time, and we pulled out to fish with the boats fairly close together.

It was as much a slanging match as a pike-fishing trip really. The Christmas spirit was still with us, and when Joe discovered that his carrier-bag contained not food but laundry, Darky fell about laughing.

He remembered the incident the following Boxing Day, too, when we met up again in the same circumstances.

'What you got for lunch today then Joe?' he yelled. 'Shirts or underpants?' And he fell about laughing again. Unfortunately he tripped over the anchor rope and fell in the lake.

To this very day I can still see Darky's wet clothes strung on a line across the two mooring poles to dry out in the frosty air while he continued to fish wearing a big overcoat.

And I can still hear the remarks Joe made every Boxing Day for the next four or five years running.

'What you doing today then Darky?' he'd say. 'Fishing— or swimming?'

Jurien Bay Incident

Two hundred or so miles north of Perth, Western Australia, lies the little fishing community of Jurien Bay. Its sea waters are sheltered, the bay is calm and shark-free and boasts two long jetties pumping fuel and fresh water to the local crayfishing boats. One of these jetties appears to be utterly barren; the water around the other teems with incredible shoals of fish. Skipjacks they are named; skippies they are called. Local and visiting anglers pack the jetty and fish with rods and handlines for those sporting (and delicious) little fish. There is a resident seal under the boards of the jetty; the biggest I have ever seen in my life. When he surfaces, the calm sea erupts and the skippies skip in terror. There are also several resident shags: huge birds, much bigger than our own in Britain, but they are streamlined, fast-moving and very accurate under water. Watching from above, it is possible, in the crystal-clear water, to see them attack the shoal on a level collision course. There is a flash of silver among the black shapes of the shoal fish below, and the shag comes to the surface to devour its freshly caught tit-bit. Hour after hour it continues. The shags' appetites are never satisfied, but their predations seem to have no effect whatsoever upon the skippy population. That shoal of fish is by far and away the largest I have seen. It must run into several hundreds of thousands.

The individual fish are eager feeders and will take small pieces of fish (shrimp in particular) readily, but there are so many small fish present in the upper layers that the larger fish below are difficult to contact. It is like trying to get through a shoal of small rudd to reach the tench below—an almost impossible task at times.

I've no idea how big skippies will grow, but I doubt if any below the jetty weigh more than half a pound. These were the ones I wanted to catch in 1978 and with my ultra-light touch-leger rod I felt I was better equipped than anyone else on the day in question.

Some anglers using big hooks and big baits would pick up the occasional good one from the bottom in 12ft of water. Their tactics avoided the small fish completely, but their heavy gear allowed them to lift out their catches without giving any sign of a bend in the rod. I wanted fish to eat, but I also wanted sport, and every time I managed to tie into one of those skippies I had a fight on my hands. True, I was bothered all the time by small pike-bait-sized fish that I didn't really want, but, with other fishing in mind, I set some aside for bait. Every so often, however, I'd get through that vast shoal of tiddlers and pick up a 'keeper' from below, which gave me a great deal of fun. I gradually filled a 'cooler' bucket with freshly caught fish, and, as the pier began to fill up with more and more anglers, bites became less frequent. It was an excellent touch-leger situation, however, and when I was able to show my catch to those who wanted to see it, I felt well satisfied that I could more than hold my own. It was like roach fishing in salt water and I am sure that, if it had been less crowded, I could have used my long rod and float tackle to even better effect. I have it in mind to do so should I ever fish there again.

Every so often, an angler, using heavier casting gear and a small fish bait, would hook a weird fish called a north-west blowfish. At that point everyone nearby 'cleared the decks' and allowed it to 'come aboard' unhindered. It would seem that these fish are inedible, deadly poisonous and highly undesirable. Those caught are killed at once by someone who knows what to do, and their ultimate end is in the crayfish pots as bait. I didn't like the look of them, nor was I impressed by their fighting qualities, which were about as fast moving as a leaky gumboot.

Three times, while I was playing a good-sized skippy, one of the shags attacked and stole my catch. The most embarrassing moment was when the shag failed to snatch the fish off the hook and became firmly attached itself. The skippy was wedged sideways-on in its throat, making its neck look like a cross. It could not or would not release it and I was forced to do battle on the surface, while the Aussies took bets on the outcome. I was in no position to back my own chances. The result was a fore-gone conclusion. Only the shag could win that contest. And it did. Fortunately the hook pulled clear and the bird came to no harm. It took about two minutes for it to manipulate the fish from crossways-on to a swallowing position, but it did so eventually and dived straight back into the attack!

At one stage I thought it might be interesting to try catching skippies on fly, and I put up an outfit with a streamer fly attached. About every third cast I felt a pluck, struck and lifted a squirming bar of silver up on to the jetty. At the first pull I was delighted, but it quickly became obvious that my small fish was foul-hooked. So was the next and the next. . . .

All of which goes to show just how many fish there are around that structure.

An orange-sized ball of 'burley' (meal and whale oil ground-bait) brought large numbers of fish out from under the jetty's shade and I would estimate that the whole lot disappeared before it had sunk a foot. Our burley was too soft to use as hook-bait, but I'm sure that a tighter mix could have been made into an acceptable paste.

Jurien Bay is the only place in the world where I have seen an angler lose the skin off two thumbs in just about as many seconds!

Tiring of skippy fishing, Ian, my host at the time, heaved out a small dead-bait using a beach-caster and multiplier. Some time later, the rod tried to take off; Ian grabbed it, clamped his thumb on the reel, and I actually saw it smoke! He yelped in pain, changed hands, ruined another completely good thumb—and then it was all over. His spool was almost empty, the fish had departed, probably not really knowing it had been hooked.

That was the fastest moving fish I have ever seen, and I often speculate even now as to what it was. There are supposedly no sharks present, and an experienced old local suggested that it could have been a kingfish weighing about a hundred pounds. Such fish occasionally moved into the bay, he said, and without a boat there was no possible hope of ever stopping them. They would keep going against the strongest tackle and rip themselves in half rather than submit to pressure. What I had just seen made me believe him.

JANUARY

In January I think mainly of pike and live-baits and dead-baits and plugs and spoons and, more than ever these days, of jigs and plastic worms. I think too of the places where I learned to use them correctly, one of them being Ottertail County, Minnesota, where I learned to appreciate ice-houses and caught perch and tulibees and crappie through ice, at times a yard thick, and snow-shoes and sleds and snowmobiles.

F.J.T.

Kid's Stuff

We were going pike fishing and we didn't have a live-bait between us. I stood outside the Royal Bucks Hospital at nine o'clock in the morning, my little box of newspapers covered over with canvas to keep out the falling snow. I used to sell papers in those days for the princely sum of half a crown, and although I needed the money badly (it paid for my hooks and other small items of fishing tackle), I always begrudged the time I had to spend in order to earn it. I wanted to be fishing with my friends who always seemed to have more money and time.

I stamped my feet and swung my arms to keep out the cold and prayed for eleven o'clock to come. Funny. I was frozen standing here with the newspapers, but I was never cold when I was fishing!

Someone whistled across the street, and Des pulled up on his old errand bike—a rod tied to the crossbar and a big live-bait can clanking in the carrier. He couldn't wait for me—and I couldn't blame him. Fishing time was too valuable to waste.

'Got the hempseed,' he said. 'I'll see you in the long pound when you're through.'

The long pound was in the arm of the local canal, and while it was not the easiest of places to fish in the dead of winter, we usually managed to get some bait-sized roach there. In those days we knew how to fish hemp reasonably well, and, although I believe it was strictly illegal, we didn't let a little thing like that worry us. The canal was nearly always deserted in winter anyway, and we weren't likely to be challenged. Des clanked off, pushing the pedals round with his heels in the manner of all errand boys, and I attended to my task of serving my customers.

By ten o'clock most of the papers were gone and most of my clients were back in the warmth of their homes—or the hospital wards from whence came the bulk of my business. The snow was falling heavily now and beginning to settle, and at that moment I rebelled! Another hour to go before I could go fishing? I could stand it no longer. I left the box and the papers for the roundsmen to pick up (that was when they paid me) and went home for my tackle.

Long before my official finishing time, I was up at the long pound fishing! The snow didn't bother me at all as I put up the long pole and the tiny porcupine quill, which I had found to be so effective for this kind of fishing.

Des already had things under control. There was great activity in the swim, and even in those cold conditions the water boiled each time a few grains of hempseed hit the surface.

I doubt very much if we hit one in ten bites, but when we both settled to fish the same swim we began to pull out small roach and gudgeon fairly regularly. And it didn't take too long to get our quota of baits.

An interesting thing happened before then, however. At that time we reckoned to use No. 16s for hemp fishing. The bites were extremely fast, and it was considered essential to use a small hook for those tiny grains. I had only one No. 16 in my tackle bag, and when the whipping on it frayed and parted (as it always did eventually), I was forced to fish with my only remaining hook—a No. 12.

I knew I'd be wasting my time, of course; No. 12s were much too big for hempseed fishing. But I was to learn differently.

The truth of the matter was that No. 12s were better on the day in question. In fact, once we had drawn the fish in close under the rod tip, they literally hooked themselves. I didn't realize it at the time, of course, but that was what was happening. The tight line from the rod tip to the bait really took care of those fast but very positive bites. When the tiny float dived under the bigger hook, meeting the resistance of the rod tip, it set itself. Striking was really only a gesture.

From then on I was sold on No. 12s for hempseed fishing and, although it is many years since I used it last, I was reminded of this incident by a Thames hemp expert a few years ago. He told me that he uses No. 10s for all his hemp fishing and that once he has the fish actively taking in the swim it is only necessary to fish with a tight line close in, and the fish will literally hook themselves.

I'm sure that was just an over-simplification of the situation on his part and that skill in the use of the seed is of prime importance. But I do see his point.

With the big can filled to capacity, but being still reluctant to go home, we put up our pike outfits. This simply meant that we removed the top joint and substituted a short, stumpy piece of wood to which had been whipped a wire tip ring! Crude— but it worked well enough.

We knew, even in those days, that if you worked up a swimful of roach there was a chance that the pike would move in to investigate. We let our gudgeon baits, tethered to eel hooks, swim around under our barrel cork floats and waited while the snow thickened. I suppose we were too anxious or too inexperienced to deal with the bites that came, for we had several pike on and lost them all. We lost some hooks too, because we had no snaps or wire traces in those days.

Towards the end of the afternoon my cork began to move away. It didn't go under but went off on a bobbing course across the canal. I called for Des to bring the net and waited and waited. The float still refused to go under, and I began to wonder if it had been a false alarm after all, but eventually I took a chance and struck. I had a fish on all right. Not a pike but a fine perch. It weighed 1lb 4oz—the biggest perch I'd ever seen—and I went home in a blaze of glory!

We kept our remaining baits and next day pedalled 11 miles through the slush and plodded our way across the snow-covered meadow. The lake was frozen, and we broke the ice to fish with our precious baits, but it was a waste of time. 'The best laid schemes. . . .' We should have gone to the canal again. I'd enjoyed that so much more.

I never received my pay for the papers that weekend and the following week I was replaced by someone more reliable! But deep down I was glad.

Just go and watch a match and see whose keep-net it is that gets attacked by pike. Isn't it nearly always the fellow who has got the roach going well?

                                                                Dick Walker

Rescue Operation

It wasn't so much a strip of bank that separated the two reservoirs as a great mountain of boulders. The water was low, and what had once been a narrow strip of land dividing the two lakes was now a wide beach with a wall of natural rock splitting it down the middle. The smaller of the two lakes boasted a boat, the larger one had no such facility, but out in the middle of it a coot was struggling in distress. It had obviously become entangled in a length of nylon fishing line and was doomed to die very unpleasantly unless something could be done.

We couldn't reach it from the bank so we moved the boat from one lake to the other, and if you think it's fun hauling a boat up what looks like a cliff face and down the other side, you should try it some time. We made it eventually, and I hauled the motor and battery across the same route. With a big landing net I caught the helpless bird and set about releasing it from its web of nylon. It had tried to peck its way free and had swallowed a great ball of monofilament in the process. Its wings and legs were tied together and it was obviously never going to get free alone, but it was in good shape otherwise.

I bit the nylon through in several places, removed the great wodge from behind its tongue, smoothed its wings, stroked its back and released it. For my pains it tried to peck my eyes out, and did in fact get me several times in the cheek, which rather hurt me. Not physically, you understand, but if that's all the thanks you get. . . .

We hauled the boat back to its original spot after watching the coot fly off, none the worse for its experience, and then we walked the area dividing the two lakes. We found two spoons, the remains of a reel-spool still containing line and several balls of nylon looking like so much green candy floss. We set fire to the line hoping we had found it all and that none of the other wild birds present would meet with the same fate as our coot.

I cannot think of a worse end for a bird than to be slowly strangled or starved in a web of nylon, and I am amazed that many anglers are still guilty of leaving nylon on the banks. It never rots and it can be just as deadly a year later as on the day it is discarded.

The nylon ensnaring our coot was in fact line that had been lost maybe two years previously when the water level was higher. Some angler had been caught up in the rocks and had pulled for a break, leaving a dozen yards of nylon still in the water. There it could do little harm, but when the water level dropped it was exposed and the wind had bunched it into a deadly ball into which the unfortunate bird had walked or flown. That was no one's fault, of course, and might be regarded as a one-off occurrence for which there is no remedy. But there is. If all wire leaders and traces used were weaker than the reel line, they would always break at that point, leaving the line intact and retrievable.

Justice

It was a cold and miserable January day when we fished one of our pike competitions at Wotton, and by mid-day most members had quit and retired to the local before going home to lunch.

Dickie was our driver; his big car had housed six of us, and we were all ready to quit the moment he gave the word.

'Another ten minutes or so,' he said, 'and we'll call it a day.'

No one had had a bite at all, but someone, I forget whom, finally caught a small pike. Dickie had retired to the bushes temporarily, and while he was away one of the members wound in his tackle, hooked on the pike and let it swim off.

Dickie returned to find his float out of sight, grabbed his rod excitedly and landed the pike for the second time. No one spoke.

A few minutes later someone said, 'Ready for off then Dickie?'

And Dickie replied seriously, 'No, I think I'll stick it out now I've got 'em going.'

Cold Comfort

The outside thermometer read $-5°F$. Mild, they said, for the time of year; I should have been here last week when it was really cold!

From the window I looked out over the lake and at the spot where I had cast a fly for bluegills in the summer—and I shivered. The jetty where I had stood was now disassembled and buried beneath a deep snowdrift on the shore; the lake itself was covered with 30in of ice and 2ft of snow. The bare trees along the shoreline glistened with hoar-frost, three red squirrels played hide-and-seek among them, and the redpolls, chickadees, purple finches and a host of other small birds fed non-stop on the sunflower seeds, corn and nuts, placed strategically for them by my friends and hosts, Jack and Dorothy Vasconcellos. Without them, these tiny creatures could never have survived this cruel winter.

Out on the lake, little more than a good cast with a mark IV carp rod away, stood Jack's fish house—a 6ft by 4ft construction of insulated plywood, containing a small wood-burning stove, a wooden floor, two kitchen chairs, an ice pick, six little jigging rods, lures and (almost) all the comforts of home. I wondered how, despite insulation and wood-stove, it might be possible to avoid freezing to death—and I shivered again.

'Are you going to stand there all day, Taylor?' Jack said in my ear. 'We've got chores to do if you want to eat today.' I had insulated boots and what I considered to be warm clothing with me, and I prepared to 'do the chores', but Jack made me don thermal underwear, thick mittens, sweaters and anorak. 'You won't be cold in the ice-house,' he informed me, 'but getting there may not be too comfortable.'

And when I started out across the beaten snow track, I knew what he meant. 'We'll break you in slowly,' he grinned. 'I guess you won't be used to this yet and we'll leave the rugged outdoor

Jack Vasconcellos's ice-bound fishing house at Dent, Minnesota

stuff till later.' It is perhaps as well we did.

I felt I was frozen solid by the time I reached the shelter, and I shielded myself in the lee of the house while Jack lit the fire. One sheet of newspaper and two small sticks of kindling? That was supposed to keep us warm? There had to be some more fuel than the small bucketful of sticks we had with us surely. 'Heck no,' said Jack, 'this little lot will last all day if necessary.'

I kicked the snow off my boots and entered. The fire began to roar and Jack shut off the damper. The house began to warm up and within minutes I was peeling off clothes, desperately trying to get cool. I swear that those two sticks of wood kept us uncomfortably warm for more than an hour, and long after they had burned out we sat in shirt sleeves and fished.

Jack had drilled two big holes in the ice before siting the house and packing snow around the base outside. Now those holes were covered with a mere inch of clear ice, which he removed with the pick and scooped out with a long-handled strainer-ladle.

In the darkness of the house, the water looked clear and blue-green. I could see clearly into the ghostly luminescence and, though the bottom, at 23ft, was not visible, I could make out the shape of fish and see my jig comfortably at 18ft. It was weird, yet strangely exciting.

We lowered the tiny jigs, armed with single waxworms, into the holes and worked them steadily at depths between 15ft and 20ft, but had no response. Minutes after we started fishing the fish shadows disappeared and we were left with what appeared to be an empty hole.

'It'll be a northern (pike) or a walleye that's responsible,' said Jack. 'Let's see if we can find out for sure.' And he lowered into the hole a strange looking decoy-plug, shaped like a baby pike but bearing no hooks.

As he jigged the lure at fifteen or so feet, I watched it swim in a perfect circle, the circumference of which grew as he increased the jigging action. I felt a peck on the line and struck but, being unused to a rod less than 2ft long, I missed.

'Crappie,' said Jack. 'Perhaps they've moved in to investigate. Let's get back down there again quick.' And he hauled in the decoy lure.

He was right, and for a time we began catching crappies. I should perhaps say that Jack began catching crappies. I simply began missing crappies! But I caught on eventually and finally got the drop of them. We dropped them into a paper-lined bucket as we caught them and began to compile a bag.

Then all went quiet again.

Jack put down a heavier jig, unbaited this time and on a heavier line. We both looked into the hole for signs of action and at that moment a walleye came up from the depths and swirled at the orange jig. I saw it open its mouth, and the jig disappeared from sight, but though I sensed Jack striking to my left, I saw the jig reappear instantly as the walleye rejected it and swirled off into the darkness under the ice. I estimated that fish at around 8lb; Jack, modestly, put it at around 6lb, but whatever its weight it did not return.

The crappie did, however, and we were in business once again. Jack took a small pike a little later on 2lb test line and a small white jig. I lost one shortly afterwards but did not worry too much. I have caught pike considerably bigger elsewhere!

We did not exactly go home in a blaze of glory, but we had enough fish for dinner. Those crappies weighed around 12oz each and were good fun on the ultra-light tackle we were using, but the bluegills we had hoped for did not show up on that occasion.

Jack thought perhaps that the light was too intense and that they'd show up towards evening when we went out again.

Once again, of course, he was right. As the light began to lessen, we had a frantic hour catching (and missing and losing) bluegills. This time we really filled the bucket, and when they stopped biting the crappies appeared again.

It was an exciting day for me, and I shall never understand how so much light manages to penetrate 2ft of snow and illuminate the water beneath that great layer of ice. I have always said that catching fish you can see is more fun than fishing blind, and, for a great part of the time, I found myself on my knees peering into the water to watch the bites as they occurred. It says a lot for the clarity of Ottertail County lakes that you can see it all happening at 18ft. I never tired of the fishing or the fish. Caught in ice-cold water, dressed and cooked within hours of being caught, those bluegills and crappies are truly fit only 'for anglers and honest men'.

And as we sipped our after-dinner bourbon that night, Jack sprang the surprise upon me. 'Today you have seen how it is in the ice-house,' he said. 'Now we'll start to think about it in terms of the great outdoors.

'Tomorrow we will put on snow-shoes, and trek out across the snow, pulling the old sled behind us. We'll need an ice-auger, rods, stools, buckets and a fair amount of tackle, and if you have the courage and the stamina, you can sit it out and fish in the open for perch, or bass or walleyes or whatever else chooses to come along.

'Tomorrow we'll see how you stand up to real ice fishing.'

I drifted off to sleep that night wondering what the next day would bring me, and it seemed that I had hardly closed my eyes when Jack nudged me into wakefulness.

According to U.S. daylight-saving time, it was eight o'clock in the morning, but still as dark as the inside of a cat. Jack looked at the outside thermometer and declared it to be much warmer than yesterday. 'It's 5° *above* zero today,' he said. 'And it looks like being a very nice morning. Look at the sky yonder.'

I looked across the dark lake and could faintly see signs of red light breaking through the base of the bare trees opposite, but at that moment I was more concerned with the great platter of bacon and eggs Jack's wife, Dorothy, had set before me. I felt that if I was going to be out long I would be burning up a few calories, and I intended that there should be plenty there for me to burn!

Daylight came with the third cup of black, fragrant coffee such as only the Americans can make, and, as the sun filtered through the snow-white trees, Jack decided it was warm enough to fish outside.

133

The ice-auger makes short work of ice up to 40in thick

'We'll forget the snow-shoes for the time being,' he said. 'We'll go perch fishing with Frank Wahldieck on Ottertail Lake instead. He's expecting us sometime this week if the weather's suitable.'

I struggled into a snowmobile suit, insulated boots and mitts, which was not easy in view of the enormous amount of clothing

I had on already, but I knew I would be glad of their protection later.

Frank was at the door when we arrived. I had ridden in Jack's car with the heater on but my feet were already beginning to feel cold. My insulated boots, though perfectly adequate for any conditions I'd ever encountered in England, simply were not up to the task here.

The snowmobile roared into life as Frank pulled the lanyard, and I mounted the pillion seat while Jack climbed into the little covered-in trailer sled behind with the tackle and ice-auger. That was my first trip on a snowmobile and it scared me half to death for a start. Later I drove it, and other machines, over great drifts of frozen snow, and across the big exposed snow-covered lakes because, apart from snow-shoes, which I did, in fact, have to wear several times, the snowmobile was the only practical form of transport.

A mile out from the shore, which was, of course, indistinguishable anyway because of the snow cover, Frank cut the motor and hauled out the power-auger. The little engine fired first pull, and the razor-sharp drill bit deeply into the ice beneath the snow. As it churned and laboured slightly under strain, great flurries of ice and snow corkscrewed upwards. The blade bit deeper, until the tiny engine was almost into the upper snow layer; then there came a surge of slush and a swirling wave of water. In about ten seconds, probably less, there was a clean smooth hole through 30in of solid ice, and within a minute there were two more alongside it!

We scooped out the frozen snow, the slush and the ice particles, and cleared the holes for fishing. I sat in the lee of the little sled and began to jig my lure just off the 18ft-deep bottom. My toes were now separated by small films of ice (that's how it felt anyway), and my ears were numb despite their wool covering. A wind in the region of 15 m.p.h. had sprung up, which, according to the American wind-chill factor chart, was having much the same effect as a drop in temperature to about − 30°F. In anyone's language that really ought to be too cold to go fishing, but I carried on because the other two did not complain. If they were hoping to make the old limey cry 'uncle' they were going to be mistaken! And the incredible thing about it was we caught fish. Not big fish, but lots of them. Yellow perch they were, very similar to our own native perch but with, I believe, one extra stripe. I tried to take photographs, Jack tried too, but it was all very difficult with heavy gloves and streaming eyes. The small floats we were using were soon coated with layers of ice. Big beads formed on the line and pretty soon we were reduced to hand-lining the fish up because the rod rings were frozen solid.

We kept most of the fish because they were pretty well frozen by the time they were unhooked, but if we were quick about it and the hook came out easily, it was just possible to return them and watch them swim back down the hole.

I told Frank that we almost invariably kept our perch in keep-nets until the end of the session, because a returned or lost perch often meant that the rest of the shoal followed it as it left the area. He expressed surprise at this, but agreed that it probably accounted for the lack of bites from time to time and the need to drill fresh holes every now and then. We had several moves during the morning—each fresh hole producing another small crop of fresh perch—and we fished hard until both Jack and Frank agreed that it was no longer fun. I thought they were never going to admit it, but I was glad when they did!

A few hundred yards from our last hole, Frank had a big ice-house situated over a large spearing hole. This was where he speared pike throughout the permitted period from time to time and also fished for perch and walleyes when they showed. We adjourned there and Frank lit the stove.

Within seconds the big house warmed up, and I began to feel civilized once more as I removed my boots and played footsie with the fire. The fish could wait and, chilblains or not, I was about to get de-iced!

Outside I heard the auger roar into life again. There was room for only two people to fish in the house and Jack was still drilling holes in the open. I suppose there was no way he could quit. Cold or not, Jack is never happy unless he is fishing, and no amount of ice or cold would ever make the slightest difference to his plans. Of all the anglers I have met, he is just about the deadliest and most efficient, and yet at the same time he is never too serious. If he caught a hundred fish he would still enjoy the last as much as the first. He never gets bored and just bubbles with enthusiasm with every catch. He is the same summer and winter alike. He catches big fish, but enjoys catching small ones just as much, and his emphasis on the fun side of fishing has undoubtedly had an influence on my own attitude during the recent years. I owe him a lot.

He carried on outside while Frank and I waited for the perch to appear inside. Once again the water was crystal clear, and I could almost count the grains of sand on the bottom in the eerie light below the ice. The whole area looked floodlit despite (or probably because of) the darkness of the house, and soon the perch moved in to investigate Frank's decoy lure.

There were fifteen of them present when we started fishing and we teased them into taking our jigs by literally bouncing them on their noses. We caught three and then I lost one.

'That's it,' I said to Frank. 'Now they'll all go.'

'Heck no,' said Frank. 'Yours went, but the others are still there. Look.'

It is true they were still there, but slowly and quite deliberately, every one of them drifted out of the immediate area along exactly the same route as the escapee. And it took fifteen minutes of decoy work to bring them back. Then the same thing happened again—twice.

I always imagined that the disappearance of a perch shoal, because of a returned or lost fish, would be a panic-stricken affair with fish bolting in all directions but it was not like that at all. These perch simply melted away into the darkness with no sign of transmitted fear. They might almost have been chub, such was their behaviour. I confess I became more interested in watching than in fishing, and I felt rather pleased with myself when Frank said, 'Well I've learned something today I hadn't figured before.'

I do not know if that is how English perch behave, of course, and I have no way of knowing if that is what happens in summer or in ordinary fishing conditions at other times of the year, but at least I was able to note many different reactions of the perch in this particular situation. And I was fascinated. I found I could tease the odd fish up almost to within a couple of feet of the surface by drawing the jig upwards through the water just out of its reach. I found that I could get bites on jigs that were hanging quite still and lifeless in the water, as long as I made them dance a little in front of an interested fish beforehand. Apart from an aquarium, I can think of no better situation for the close study of fish behaviour, and I was sorry when it was time to leave. More so when I learned that it was my turn to 'ride shotgun' on the trailer sled. There is just no way of describing a journey like that!

That night we ate fish at Frank's home, and I sampled the delights of his wife Wilma's cooking. 'The tulibee should be in,' said Frank. 'Why don't you go and see Cecil Porter? He'll put you on to them.'

Two days later we did just that. Jack left me with Cecil—and he and I fished for those fabulous Minnesotan white fish from his even smaller ice-house.

Half choked by fumes from his belching oil-stove, but nevertheless warm and comfortable, we caught several and failed to catch many more. Tulibee are herring-like fish, oily and delicious smoked. A bag of three-pounders, which we caught from another ice-house, one belonging to yet another friend, Frank Hammers, were dealt with by Frank Wahldieck next day. Never have I tasted better fish. Twelve hours in Frank's special brine solution and another twelve in the converted refrigerator/smoker, transformed them into a dish that could only be described as magnificent.

Jack and I spent my last two days catching crappie. They had suddenly become difficult to locate, and Jack had drilled many holes outside without success. Eventually, however, they came to us. We hauled the sled across the snow a mere 200 yards from his home on the bank, and there they were in abundance. Jack was of the opinion that, far from scaring the fish, drilling

A crappie catch from below the ice

holes in the ice eventually attracted them. This seemed to be the case, and it is reasonable to assume that fish might well be drawn towards an air hole.

Fishing outside could never be as pleasant as house fishing but, on those days when the crappie obliged, it was an exciting change. Crappie tend to suspend at one level. Find that level and bites are almost guaranteed—bites that pull the rod tip down to the water surface. This is often true of both summer and winter fishing, and our 'final fling' crappie lived up to their reputation.

Wearing mittens and gauntlets to protect our hands from frost-bite, we popped those crappie through the ice one after another. We kept them all. So cold was the air that the fish stiffened as they left the water and were almost deep frozen within minutes. They would have been dead long before they could be unhooked and returned!

I have, on the odd occasion, fished through ice in Britain. I have broken thin ice with stones and have hacked holes through thick ice in years gone by, but I had never really *enjoyed* ice fishing until I went to Ottertail County, Minnesota. I would dearly love to believe that I will be doing it again before too many years have passed.

FEBRUARY

*In February I recall full dykes, blizzard roach and chub
. . . and I murmur to myself that the coarse-fish season is
coming to an end yet again.*

F.J.T.

Rubbish Rafts and Chub

It was a very cold day in February, and I was fishing for chub
on the upper Ouse. The margins were fringed with ice, and the
banks were hard with frost. Altogether it wasn't a very pleasant
day to be out at all, but as always, one had to make the best of
available time.

A week earlier the river had been in spate, and a whole lot of
dead reeds and rushes had been washed down together with an
accumulation of other flood-water rubbish. Most of it had
passed on downstream and out of the way, but just below
where I was sitting, the branches of a sallow bush leaned out
over the river and trailed into the water. At this point a whole
raft of rubbish had been held up by the trailing branches, and
an area of several square yards was completely covered. The
water at this point seemed to be almost dead still, and because I
had seldom, if ever, caught chub in the slacks of this river, I
was legering out well away from it, on the edge of the main
current.

Somehow, I'm not sure how, a loose piece of bread crust found its way into the water and drifted down on the surface to come to rest on the edge of the raft of rubbish.

I remember thinking that, if it had been summer and this had been a carp lake, I might have expected that piece of crust to disappear! I even thought, perhaps, that it might have been taken by chub in summer, though this was not an accepted chub-fishing method here. Chub were known to take floating crust on the Hampshire Avon; indeed we had taken plenty that way from the middle reaches. Not here though; the chub would not come to the top for floating crust here even in summer; and they wouldn't come to the top for crust anywhere in winter. Or would they?

It seemed that my ideas were quite wrong, for out of the corner of my eye I saw the raft bulge slightly. A pair of lips appeared and there was a swirl as the crust disappeared. This, on a cold winter's day, was quite out of keeping with what I thought I knew about chub, but it didn't take me long to replace that piece of crust with another piece holding a hook!

I was surprised to find that, despite what I thought about the water being slack at that point, there was quite a strong current pulling under the raft. Had I given the matter any thought at all I should have realized this had to be so anyway, but seeing a seemingly stationary raft of rubbish had given me the impression of still water.

Within half an hour I had action. A chub of nearly 4lb came to the top, took my piece of crust and was soon bullied into the net. That, I thought, is that. There will be no more chub left under there now, and if there are any, they'll be pretty well scared.

But it wasn't so. Shortly afterwards I had another chub on another piece of floating crust from exactly the same spot. Then I began to wonder about this particular situation. Undoubtedly it was contrary to all my chub-fishing doctrine, and I was a little confused. I'd always expected chub to prefer baits presented very close to the bottom in these conditions and, even after two surface fish, I still felt that this was basically right.

142

But this incident had at least proved to me that chub were likely to hole up under these rubbish rafts, and so I began to search for some more—this time with a leger.

I caught another five chub from underneath the sallow bush; a remarkable catch by the standards expected of that little stretch of river! I only once remember exceeding that number, and on that day, in very similar circumstances, I had eleven.

But I learned quite a lot about chub fishing on the day I have just described.

First, I found out that there's very often a lively current underneath some of these held-up rubbish rafts, and it has always been my experience that chub prefer water with at least a hint of lively current nearby. Second, of course, I learned that chub will sometimes take floating crust in winter, and in later years I found this to be true of waters other than the Ouse. The trouble is that I have, so far, been unable to recognize the conditions in which they are most likely to do so. There seems to be no common factor, but I should add that there are stretches of the Thames where chub can be induced to take floating crust almost at any time. Peter Stone and some of the members of the Oxford Specimen Group have got this off to a fine art. They spend a long time 'feeding' a stretch right under the opposite bank with loose crusts, and then, when the chub begin to show, they take them on relatively fine tackle.

Third, I learned of the peculiar fondness chub have for these rubbish rafts. They seem to like to have a 'roof' over their heads, and, at least on the waters I fish, I think one of the most likely post-flood chub swims is one such as I have described. Over a mile or so of river many of these 'sanctuaries' form throughout the winter, and I think they're well worth exploiting.

Fool's Errand

A thin layer of snow covered the ground. The wind blew clouds of white dust into the headlights half an hour or so before the Hampshire dawn, and I pulled off the road briefly to avoid its hypnotic effect. Hot tea from the thermos steamed up the inside of the car, and as I wiped the windows clear I wondered what kind of fool it is who gets up at this time of day to travel in cold darkness towards an even colder dawn for the chance of catching a fish he intends to put back again. But opportunities to fish certain waters come infrequently, and one must accept them when they do come in order to be sure of future offers. To accept an invitation to fish and then fail to turn up would not only be discourteous, it could also prevent someone else from enjoying the privilege. There are fewer opportunities than anglers, and hogging a date that someone else might well be pleased to accept is rightly frowned upon. Even so, I did not rate my chances very highly. The sudden drop in temperature, the snow and the low water did not exactly have me hopping about with enthusiasm. I could think of other things I might be happier doing, and, after covering the last few miles slowly so that my arrival coincided with daylight, I found myself a little reluctant to leave the warmth of the car.

I was alone. No one else was on the water; no one had travelled with me, and, as I was not very familiar with the fishery, I left my tackle and took a brisk walk along the bank. Chub, dace, grayling and roach, my host had told me. Some big fish of all species but none of them easy to locate, and I tried to figure it out as I walked.

In all I spent nearly two hours trying to make up my mind about where to fish, and, although I cannot claim any enormous success, I believe my strategy was the right one.

It is very easy, on a new water, to settle for the first attractive-looking swim without giving the matter much thought; and to come unstuck doing so.

I believe that in order to look a water over properly, it is advisable to do so without tackle. Later, the tackle can be put to use finding out more about the depth and nature of the bottom, but for a start I think you tend to pay more attention to detail if the rods are left behind.

When, years ago, I had a lot more time at my disposal, I often used to boast that I spent most of my first day at any new water without putting a rod together. I am sure I was right then, and I would still practise it today if I had the time. Time spent just looking is never, in my opinion, time wasted. If you take all day to figure out something and end up catching fish in the last hour, you have achieved as much as the angler who has flogged away thoughtlessly all day with the same result.

I finally settled for a lively little swim on a wide bend. The current set diagonally across the bend, pulling the float tackle away nicely from my bank, and I figured it for a swim likely to hold any or all of the species mentioned.

White maggots and a loaf of bread were the only baits I had and, after trotting through for half an hour, fiddling around with the depth and feeding steadily, I had my first bite. A small grayling took about half-way down the swim, backed off against the rod pressure and, helped by the current, came off after showing briefly. It was too small to keep and would have gone back anyway, so I wasn't very much concerned, despite my liking for grayling.

Usually, where there is one grayling there are others, and I began to think, after missing two more bites on the trot, that I had been thinking along the right lines. The cold morning, the nature of the swim, the small bait (i.e., single maggot) and bites from grayling, all tied in together. And I was pleased that the bites came at almost exactly where I had expected them. Which just goes to show how wrong you can be sometimes. That particular honey-hole did not produce another bite all day!

What happened was that by a stroke of luck I found some roach farther down the swim at the tail end. A raft of floating debris was held up by an overhanging hawthorn bush in a spot where the current was much slower, and a poor cast at one stage put my tackle on a line directly to it. Instead of brushing past the debris as it had been doing previously, the float caught up and was held firm. It was, in fact, in an excellent situation— one I had not judged practical before—and so I left well alone. The bait swung under the raft while the float jammed hard against it, preventing it from going further. It was a strange feeling, but somehow I *knew* the float was going to be pulled

145

under, and somehow I also knew *when* it would happen. The result was a well-timed strike and that lovely feeling of panic that always follows in those circumstances. I identified the fish as a roach before it came off, and it took me some time to manipulate the tackle back into the same spot again; but the moment I succeeded there came another bite. This time I hauled the fish out of trouble and into open water quickly.

It would bore the reader to relate my misfortunes in detail, but in fact I lost many more fish than I landed, because the combination of small hook and fine tackle was no match for a strong fish in a snaggy situation. Other factors added to the difficulty as well, and the nature of the bites soon made it apparent that I was literally pulling the hook *out* rather than *in* every time I struck. The fact that the fish were tending to back away under pressure also helped to make things more difficult. I needed a bit more line strength, I needed a slightly bigger hook, and I really needed to be able to make the strike slightly downstream rather than up. All of which added up to a much cruder float tackle, the presentation of which the fish simply would not accept, as I quickly learned for myself.

The pay-off was that I reverted to a simple leger tackle, used a line of 5lb breaking strain, a No. 10 hook and crust cubes instead of maggots. A complete turn around, but, I thought, a more positive bait presentation.

I was able, by using a little extra lead, to cast from a downstream angle and anchor my bait right under the raft. The line bowed slightly in a downstream direction, and when I struck I did it with a downstream pull.

It probably made little sense, after feeding with loose maggots, to fish with a crust hook-bait, but in the circumstances I felt it offered a better chance of a decent fish. I have learned over the years that in many situations roach prefer a comparatively small crust cube to a bunch of maggots when a bigger hook size is indicated.

I would like to report an outstanding success but, while I mastered the swim fairly well eventually, it was all a bit of an anti-climax.

I hooked and landed five fish and never missed another bite. Three were over 2lb, and the others were slightly under. Which, had they been roach, would have given me something to brag about for a long time. The trouble is, they were all chub.

Winter Night Roach

Even in the dead of winter roach often prefer to wait until night before feeding, and many specialist roach anglers insist that more good quality fish are taken in failing light than at any other time of day.

The last hour before sunset can seem a long time coming after a traditional early morning start, but in my opinion it is worth the wait. I have my doubts about dawn starts anyway. After the first brief dawn session, the middle-of-the-day hours often become boring and unproductive. Long before evening, many anglers head for home, having decided that there is little point in staying. They prefer to negotiate ditches and barbed-wire fences in daylight, and no one can blame them for that. Most coarse-fish anglers carry a lot of gear, and darkness can bring problems.

Roach fishing remains for me one of the most enjoyable and demanding of outdoor pastimes

It is, nevertheless, worthwhile planning a later start with a lot less gear and exploiting the last hour of daylight to the full. There is something rather special about the 'last knockings', and despite the coming of a sudden frost and the chilling of the night air, it is often well worth staying on for a short time, after dark too. It isn't everyone's idea of fun, but at this time of year, an hour in the dark does not mean a midnight drive home. By six o'clock in the evening the fishing is likely to be over, and, with a few simple precautions taken in advance, no discomfort need be experienced.

Wear warm clothing, take a flask of hot soup, settle in early, have everything handy (including a torch) and fish with simple leger tackle in a recognized roach swim. Don't overdo it at first. If no bites come, don't waste too much time, but do not write off the whole idea after one blank session. Roach swims do not always produce at this hour, and not every night is a good roach night.

When everything is right, however, the bold, slow bite of a big roach after dark is magic.

Rain of Silver

Ken and I fixed the little electric motor on the small punt and drifted around Sawmills Lake on a bright, mild day in early February. There was nothing serious about our fishing; we had a tiny 6ft rod each and a few very small single-hook spinners. We expected to catch pike, we expected them to be small, and we were content to leave it at that. But at the same time we were hoping that we might possibly find a few perch, which would teach us something for the future. We had picked up the odd perch from time to time when we were tench fishing in summer, but had never really laid into a shoal of them. There is a deep, gravel-bottomed hole well out into Sawmills Lake, which used to hold perch in numbers some years ago, and occasionally we had motored or drifted across it, casting and working our little lures deep the whole time.

Things turned out pretty much as we expected. We caught pike. They were small, but although we managed to catch one straggler perch, we learned nothing from it. In all we caught eleven pike when most of the water was oily calm, by casting along the edge of the slightly rippled surface halfway across the lake; and although the takes almost invariably came near the surface, there was nothing to suggest the presence of pike and no activity to suggest a particular line of cast. The water looked pretty dead, but the small pike were keen enough to feed while those conditions remained.

Then, towards noon, there came a great hatch of small, black flies, which drew thousands of small rudd to the surface. At least a quarter of the whole lake was dimpled by rising, flipping fish, and suddenly there was a great eruption in one corner as a pike ploughed its way through the shoal. I have seen this happen hundreds of times before, but I cannot remember ever seeing so many small fish hurl themselves out of the water at the same time. It made a sound like someone throwing in a bucketful of gravel, and hundreds of tiny fry seemed to hang in mid-air before dropping back like silver rain into the water.

I have no idea how big the pike was, but naturally enough I wanted it, and both Ken and I competed with each other to reach it next cast. While we were doing so there was another great eruption behind us, quite near the boat, and another rain of silver poured back into the water.

It was very much like chasing rainbows (or surface carp in summer). Wherever we were casting it was a safe bet that the activity would take place somewhere else, and eventually we stopped fishing and just watched. As soon as we saw a disturbance we pitched our baits in, but it was so much wasted effort. More often than not we were out of range, but on the few occasions when we were on target our offerings were ignored.

It is not an unusual state of affairs, of course, and it certainly did not surprise us that we did not get a hit, but that did not prevent us from trying. The atmosphere was one of suspense and excitement, and although I suppose we both knew it was not 'on', we kept pegging away. It is very hard not to in these circumstances.

149

We chased those will-o'-the-wisp pike for two hours or more, never knowing whether they weighed two pounds or twenty because, despite their near-surface strikes, they never once showed. It could, I suppose, have been the same pike all the time, but I doubt if one lone fish would have bothered to cover such a wide area with such an abundant food supply all around.

It was an interesting session despite the frustration, and it was not until I was on the way home that I recalled the techniques used in the United States for bass in the same situation. At certain times of year, vast shoals of tiny shad collect near the surface, and in the early morning sunlight the bass tear into them in exactly the same way as those pike were hounding our rudd. The problems of being in the right spot at the right time are identical, but the American fishermen nail the bass on surface lures. They catch and twitch their shiny metallic floating plugs in the immediate vicinity of each strike and are ready at all times to pick up and cast when the water erupts again and more tiny fish come flying out.

Of course, the idea of using surface plugs never occurred to me at the time, although I have used them successfully so many times in Arkansas and other states. I was too busy throwing the spinners that had already accounted for pike that morning, and in any event I had no surface plugs with me!

It is astonishing how fortunes can change during the course of a day's pike spinning, and had I been geared up for serious fishing I would have taken along a lot more lures than I did. Then I could have tried different sizes and colours, and I might just have thought about surface-lure fishing in time. I am convinced it would have worked.

For the next few days it rained solidly, and, as its level rose, the water became murkier. When Ken and I went pike fishing the following week we were prepared for all eventualities, and we took along a supply of dead-baits as well as a great selection of lures. The water was running over the top of the dam as thick as cocoa, and, although the day was bright and mild, we knew from the start that we were going to be out of luck. We do not rate our chances very high in dirty water.

150

There are odd times when a lone old pike may locate a legered dead-bait and take it, but generally speaking I regard piking as a waste of time in those conditions.

We gave it a couple of hours and then decided there were better things to do. We were on our way home as some of the other members were arriving. They ribbed us a bit for quitting early, of course, but we learned later that they had fared no better than we had.

Sawmills Lake, apart from when it has been churned up by winds and made dirty by flood drainage, is an exceptionally clear lake, which is probably why it responds to spoon and plug fishing so well. Our thinking has perhaps changed in this respect in recent years.

There was a time when I believed (and a good many books suggested) that pike could easily distinguish between an artificial and a real bait in gin-clear water, and that a certain anount of colour was needed for successful spinning.

I do not think that way any more. I believe that there is more chance of a pike spotting a plug or spoon from a distance if the water is clear. And a mental round-up of all the pike waters I fish establishes one clear and undeniable fact: the ones that can be relied upon to produce pike to artifical lures are all extremely clear.

It is well known that some waters are regarded as 'good spinning waters'; others are considered an absolute waste of time. Many anglers have written to me over the years wanting to know why the pike in the waters they fish never seem to take spoons or plugs. I have also been told of waters that will produce pike in summer but not in winter.

Obviously I do not know the answers to all their problems. Without fishing their waters I would not have a chance, and, even if I could fish them, I would still have to do a lot of guessing.

It does seem to me, however, that pike takes lure better in waters that are for the most part clear.

There are times when clear waters turn dirty, and there are times when dirty waters suddenly go clear—which means there is just a chance that lures may work in the worst of waters occasionally, but the odds are probably too great to be serious about it in many cases. And, of course, the sudden clearing of an otherwise coloured water may well be due to an overnight, severe frost or a prolonged cold spell, both of which may go a long way towards discouraging pike from chasing lures.

I know of at least one water that never actually clears until January, by which time the pike have slowed down considerably anyway. On the whole, I think it's a safer bet to stick to real fish in these waters. Anyone fond of winter spinning and plug fishing (as I am), will, I am sure, do better in very clear, still waters of good depth.

In the United States, where lure fishing has reached standards higher than anywhere else in the world, the finest game waters are gin clear. Which is why the Americans get so uptight about carp. They make waters dirty and spoil the lure fishing.

'February Filldyke' ought to read 'February fill pike'.
Don Wray

MARCH

In March I can think only that the season is about over and that three months must pass before I can coarse fish again. But I can think of trout and salmon and sea fishing in the meantime . . . and of the garden and the plans for next June.
F.J.T.

Final Fling

It was to be the last pike-fishing trip of the season, and, while I am prepared to rough it occasionally, I felt it was time to have a little comfortable fishing for a change. I was not really out for blood. If I had been that way inclined, I would have treated the whole session more seriously. I might have searched the water in a small boat, spent some time with the sonar unit, perhaps baited with a few sprats in advance and generally put in more effort. Then I might have caught nothing at all, and my last piking trip of the season would have been a washout. As it was, I cared little whether I caught anything or not that day, because it was to be an exercise in comfort and in seeing just what you can do to make life more tolerable on an exposed lake.

Out came the big pontoon on Sawmills Lake and on board went the tackle, the bait, the essential brewing-up materials, the food, the gas heater, the electric motor and the portable T.V.

Well why not? Gerry Hughes and I were the only two people on the lake, and we were unlikely to disturb anyone else, so I saw no harm in it. Besides, it was fun. There is nothing to suggest that if I had been anchored in the same spot in a little cockle-shell of a boat, exposed to the wind and weather, watching my tackle like a hawk, I would have caught any more fish than I did. And I am sure I would have enjoyed it far less.

The big pontoon takes some man-handling into position, but surprisingly the little electric motor, which runs off a 12-volt car battery, moved it against a stiff breeze and held it while the poles were driven into place. That same battery ran the T.V., of course.

So, with carpet slippers on and good strong tea brewed, we sat back in the deck-chairs with two dead-baits out and waited for the action to begin. The wind was blowing from behind, the canopy was at 'half mast', and the little gas heater gradually warmed up the inside of the boat. Two indicators hung down from the fishing rods, which were placed so that we could see movement easily, and after a hard week we were completely relaxed. Who cared very much about fish anyway? We'd both caught some before!

I admit that I did not really watch T.V. seriously. It was a fair enough picture, but by daylight there are so many other things to see. Wotton Lakes are well known for their wild bird life, and I found the antics of grebes and mallards and coots and moorhens and Canada geese much more interesting than mid-day chat programmes; but there have been times since when that little set has proved useful in the fishing hut, caravan, tent or boathouse at other, distant waters.

It will never be used in the dead of night where other anglers are seriously fishing for carp or other species, of course. Like pressure lamps, transistor radios and cassette recorders, portable T.V. sets have no place at the water's edge when serious fishing is afoot.

I was not really dozing when the dolly went up and line began to strip off the spool. I was just feeling warm and mellow, and to be truthful not wanting to be troubled by a lot of fishy activity, but I picked up the rod and did the necessary. Which was perhaps just as well, because the pike had decided to double back and try to wrap itself around one of the poles. It came clear eventually and, against my better judgement, I put the big landing net under it and hauled it aboard. That is when it finally came to life, of course, and it wrapped itself into an unholy mess of treble hook, wire trace, net mesh and teeth, which took an age to unravel. So much so that I had to hold the fish upright in the water for some time to allow it to recover. I have said it a hundred times before, and I will still say yet again: I simply cannot see that a net has any humane advantage over a gaff that is used with care and precision. After that, I left the net where it was and put up the small collapsible gaff.

Strangely enough, the next fish fought harder and longer than any I had caught in recent weeks, and when I drew it to the boat I could see immediately that it had been expertly gaffed under the chin quite recently by someone else. I slipped my gaff in the same small hole and released the fish in seconds. It swam off at once, none the worse for wear.

We took only three pike that day, the best a twelve-pounder, which came soon after lunch, but of course there was more to it than catching fish. On a water like Sawmills Lake there are other factors that, though strictly connected with fishing, do not necessarily need great catches of fish to make them enjoyable. I do not mean to wax poetical, but I feel so very close to nature there knowing, as I do, that everything possible has been done to ensure that man's intensive efforts to squeeze every last ounce out of the surrounding land has not endangered the wild life species present.

And, of course, there are the memories; for it was at Wotton that it all began to happen for me!

On the Rocks

The coarse-fish season had just ended; Kenny and Dumps and Lofty and Dennis were all with me in the bar of the hotel down on the Lizard Peninsula; and we were talking fishing. Kenny is

155

Dennis the Menace, on the rocks at Lizard Point

a Buckinghamshire man like me, but he lives down on the Lizard now. The others were Cornishmen to the core and all interested in fishing. They soon had me figured for a 'river fisher' and not a sea angler, but our interests were much the same. It made me smile when, to a man, they insisted that they were only concerned with catching fish to eat. They weren't really bothered about the sporting aspect at all. Fish were to be caught for eating, they told me, not for any other reason. Then, almost in the same breath, they told me that they often went fishing for wrasse 'just for something to do', and that, although they kept a few occasionally for the lobster pots, they usually put them back! They float fished off the rocks and legered from the beaches, fished the night through many times and went to work next morning and, when conditions were fair, they took their small boats out for bass and mackerel.

It was late March when I was there; I had only a weekend to spare between seasons, and, although I am no sea fisher, I took what tackle I could that I thought might be useful at a push.

The wind was in the east, it was cold and there were no fish about, but, as Dumps said at the time, 'You can always catch wrasse and if you want to have a go we'll take you tomorrow.' I wanted to have a go and said so, and, when they pointed out the rocks in the distance where we'd have to go, I didn't take too much notice. They looked like any other rocks to me. Not too big and easy to climb down. But I should have taken more notice of the way they were chuckling into their pints of bitter.

'Be here at half past one,' said Dennis. 'If you're not there, we go without you.' And I thought, at last, here were people after my own heart. That is my way too. I wait for no man; if he has set a time he should stick to it and allow for traffic jams and hold-ups. I may not be a sea fisher but, I thought, at least I have something in common with these fellows.

I was on time, but it wasn't all that long before I was wishing I'd been late!

I expected sea fishing from the rocks to be different and, indeed, having tried it before off Fowey and caught congers, I knew it would be, but I never expected to have to climb 150ft down a cliff face and generally try to think like a mountain goat!

I had a haversack full of gear (not knowing what I would require), and when my rubber boot slipped on the first step, and I looked down to where I had nearly fallen, I froze. 'There's no way you'll get me down there,' I said. 'I'll stay up here and watch.' And I meant it. Now I knew the reason for those sly looks in the bar.

Kenny, who is about my age and half as heavy again, shamed me. He just clambered down that cliff-face as if he had been doing it every day of his life, and my pride was shattered. Scared or not, I had to go down; so I shut my eyes and went.

To be fair, Dennis carried my rod and my bag, otherwise I never would have made it. I just hung on to my camera and hoped; Dennis, meanwhile, delighted to have something to moan about, kept harping on about the 'amount of tackle some blokes carry'.

The big rock was flat, and there was plenty of room when we finally made it. I tucked myself in out of the wind, convinced that the only way I'd ever get back up was via the coastguard helicopter. At least that thought made me feel good!

My glass carp rod was not really the best tool for fishing 20ft above the water, but it answered, and when I figured out the geography of the bottom a bit and found the clear spots, I dispensed with the float and legered out as far as I could throw.

Dennis hooked a big fish on his powerful rod and began cranking it in at high speed when his reel folded up on him. A nut had come loose somewhere and the result was that whatever fish it was got off. My rod, just about then, was nearly pulled from my hand, and I hit into a big fish too, which I began handling as I would pike or carp.

'Keep it coming,' Dennis yelled. I pumped and hauled, but it was too late. Whatever it was wrapped itself into a great load of seaweed, and I had to break.

Dumps told me I ought not to have stopped winding but should have kept cranking away to keep the fish coming. 'An inch of slack here,' he said, 'and they'll snag you in a second.' I could see what he meant, but I cannot think how I could have hauled more on that fish with my inadequate tackle.

But I did manage to do so next time I had a bite. I just kept the fish coming and skulldragged it out and up the rockface on my 15lb line. It was a wrasse and weighed just over 3lb— undoubtedly a great deal smaller than the one I'd lost previously. But it was first blood to me! We hooked, landed and lost several other fish that afternoon, and when our lugworms ran out we tried limpets with no success.

The sun was warm, the view was magnificent and I felt at peace. Until someone reminded me that I'd got to climb all the way up that cliff again!

But while I fished I had been watching Dumps and Dennis literally running up and down, here and there, trying new spots, and it seemed to me that, although these two were born and bred to it, they were not the kind of people to risk falling into that churning cauldron and being smashed to bits on the rocks below. It was, I suppose, a simple question of confidence, and when I thought about it calmly, I realized that it was no more dangerous for me than for them. And I scrambled up to the top without so much as a pause or a downward glance. Dennis carried my tackle again though, which gave him the chance to complain again.

They told me afterwards that this particular rock was a special one. There was only the one way down and a difficult one at that, but it meant that those who knew the route could be sure of getting a spot during the summer when all the easy rocks were occupied by visitors. I cannot blame them for that, and suppose I should regard it as a privilege that they showed it to me at all. Not that I would ever have found it again anyway.

I am aware, of course, that without the aid of Dumps and Dennis, I never would have caught a fish, but as mine was the biggest I couldn't resist a bit of a leg-pull. 'Takes an ole river fisher,' I said. 'Some blokes would keep on about it, but I'm not that sort.'

In the crowded bar that night I said nothing. I had enjoyed a grand afternoon and leg-pulls were out. Then someone said, 'Who had the biggest fish today?'

I kept quiet, but Dumps said, 'Tell 'em, Fred.' And Dennis said, 'Yes, tell 'em Fred.' So I told 'em.

At which the landlord said, 'In that case, old chap, it's pints all round on you. Old Cornish custom. That's handsome that is!' I ought to have known!

159

Reading Matter

The close season is also the time for reading and thinking, the one invariably running concurrently with the other.

Of all the angling authors whose work (unlike the majority in my library) I have read from cover to cover over and over again, Sheringham stands out as the greatest. An expert in all fields of angling, a thoughtful man who wrote with a simple modesty that belied his expertise, Sheringham paid no heed to those who regarded game fishing as a superior sport to coarse or sea fishing. He loved all branches of it and could write of success or failure with equal enthusiasm. He also believed in luck — which would probably not go down too well with today's specimen hunters and matchmen!

The truth is, however, that while skill, observation and attention to detail are undoubtedly more to be relied upon than luck for consistent results today, there are times when it *does* play a part. And we should be thankful that it does. I know I am!

Sheringham wrote in 1911 that:

> So far as my experience goes, it is certain that good luck is the most vital part of the equipment of him who would seek to slay big carp. For some men I admit the usefulness of skill and pertinacity; for myself, I take my stand entirely on luck. To the novice I would say cultivate your luck. Prop it up with omens and signs of good purport. Watch for magpies in your path. Throw salt over your left shoulder. . . .

And he went on to say that these things were important in carp fishing. Serious carp men who have not read Sheringham might well be offended by such remarks; serious carp men who have read Sheringham will not. They will know that this was tongue-in-cheek stuff written by one who was well aware of the difficulties of carp fishing and who had caught them.

He regarded a ten-pounder as a big fish, and, while the situation may have changed considerably since those days, the truth is that a 10lb carp is still a big fish. It does not warrant much mention in the angling press today, but carp enthusiasts still make records of their 'doubles' each season. They catch more per season than Sheringham caught in his lifetime, but modern tackle and the fact that there are now a great many more carp to be caught account for that. And, of course, in those days there were few, if any, specialist carp fishers.

It was a slow game then and few people regarded it as worth-while.

'You cannot fish for carp in half a day,' said Sheringham. 'It takes a month!'

Nor was he alone in thinking so. Some twenty years later, Patrick Chalmers said it was better to 'forget the carp entirely and some day you will catch him on a lobworm when you are fishing for barbel or bream'. He was writing of Thames carp, of course, but he later described how to start carp fishing in August with a view to catching your carp in September!

Perhaps he was influenced by Sheringham, for elsewhere he quotes Sheringham's Carp Table as being:

> One day   = 18 hours (summer time)
> 18 hours   = 1 potato
> Ten years = 1 carp

And it appears that, in keeping with other earlier writers, both authors pinned their faith in potato baits, although Sheringham wrote with authority of honey pastes, surface crust and other baits.

Tackle in those days was different, cruder and less reliable, but the approach was similar inasmuch as the carp was considered to be cunning, easily alarmed, difficult to catch but possible to 'educate'. And that is pretty much how it is today.

Nevertheless, when you consider the advances made in other fields, more progress has been made with carp than with all the other species.

It is interesting to read the little refinements considered necessary in those days for roach, dace and chub, and to realize that we employ much the same ideas today. We can scale down with finer tackle and more delicately balanced floats, but there is very little new in the way of basic bait presentation today compared with earlier this century. Baits are similar, except that we probably use even fewer today than anglers did then, and it might pay us from time to time to try out some of the old ones again. Like macaroni for chub, and caddis grubs for roach and dace, for instance.

What appears to have happened is that we have reduced our roach, dace and chub baits to a minimum (in many waters maggot and caster are the only baits used at all), whereas we have increased the number of proven carp baits enormously. (This is also true, perhaps, of tench, though probably with less impact generally.)

We began carp fishing (or at least I did) by allowing freeline all the time to a taking carp—either by stripping from a centre-pin or opening a fixed-spool bale arm, but we have learned since that it is sometimes better not to. We pinned our faith on potatoes and bread and very little else. (I remember a very early carp-fishing trip when I was told by an old farmer that 'bread were never no good 'ere. You need pertaters biled in sugar'.) Today, while these are still good baits, experiments with a great many more have brought success on hard-fished waters.

The triangle, or treble hook, is no longer regarded as right and proper, nor is it considered necessary. The old exponents of carp fishing would seldom have used a No. 2 single for a potato bait. Using a line of 10lb or more breaking strain with the hook tied direct was unheard of, and probably inadvisable anyway, because modern monofilament had not yet been invented. Silkworm gut had to serve for the terminal tackle, tied to a reel line of dressed silk, and there was always the need for compromise.

'The carp themselves prefer fine gut,' quoth Sheringham, 'but where you are likely to get hold of a big one I advise you to disregard their preference!' Beautifully put. He was aware of all the problems; we are fortunate in that we can do more about them.

I never at any time regarded carp fishing as a month-long sojourn, but I have many times fished for a week and, on one occasion, for eleven days, without really expecting to catch one.

Today, with more waters well stocked with fish in the double-figure category, I can go off for an afternoon or even a short two-hour session and *expect* to catch a fish. I am disappointed if I fail, but only because my circumstances are more favourable. I certainly do not regard myself as a better carp fisher. And even though my bites come more frequently and I see surface carp activity much more often, I still look upon carp in much the same way as Sheringham. I still experience excitement, frustration, disaster, panic—and luck.

But I do not go carp fishing convinced that 'nothing will happen to disturb me'. That is the big difference.

Today we meet with situations where big carp are few and far between (and bites even fewer and farther), but most of us know waters where we can catch several fish each season if we have a mind to. We are blessed with better rods, better tackle, better techniques, better approaches. We have more well-stocked waters, more and bigger carp to catch. We are not scared of them any more, and we refuse to believe they cannot be caught.

And we differ too in one more important respect. Having caught our carp we put it back to grow bigger and to become even more difficult to catch next time. The same could not be said for the carp of Sheringham's time. They were knocked on the head with a degree of satisfaction, and presumably eaten with relish.

It is possible that carp fishing today would hold fewer problems if we did the same thing—but that doesn't bear thinking about!

> *15 March does not come too soon for the perch. If the season were to go on for another week, you could sit over any deep hole on this river (Hampshire Avon) and pull perch dripping with spawn to the bank all day.*
>
> *For those who want heavy keep-nets, no matter what the cost, or the income from a fishing net with no thought of the future, that's fine. But the majority of us, who would conserve to enjoy later, should speak against this talk of doing away with the close season.*
>
> *Tom Williams*

Should Auld Acquaintance . . .?

Luggy and I grew up together when we were kids and learned to fish the nearby River Thame for roach and perch at the same time as we learned to swim. In fact we more often than not left the rods to fish for themselves while we dived in elsewhere to cool off. Those summer days were always hot and it never rained that I can remember!

He moved down to the Lizard some years ago. He was, he said, fed-up with fighting London's traffic, breathing petrol fumes and competing in the rat race. Only a rat, he said, could win a rat race and *that* was no great achievement.

Today a fitter (if somewhat fatter) man, he lives an uncomplicated life, which revolves round a stone cottage, a vegetable garden, a fishing rod, some lobster pots and a beachcomber's eagle eye. He is the perfect example of what I would call a happy man. I envy him his courage and his ability to make such a decision so early in life. Deep down, I knew that this was what *I* really wanted to do, but because I was too deeply involved in other things I did not make the same kind of move until years later.

It is, however, a great advantage to have someone like Luggy around when I decide to visit Cornwall and fish a spell. Over the years he has learned the rocky coastline (you can almost cast into the sea from his back garden), and he knows how to wriggle down and struggle up those sheer cliffs with a degree of safety. And he has a fair idea of what our chances are going to be before we set out to fish.

We talked of those old days when we fished together again in that entirely different spot; we reminisced but did not indulge in the swimming because the setting was hardly right for it. The cold north-east wind blew across the Lizard point, and it was only when we had negotiated the gentle climb down to Canker Drang behind the shelter of the big rocks that we began to feel the warmth of the sun.

I have fished the Cornish rocks from time to time over a great many years and have caught pollack, wrasse, mackerel, bass and conger from them during light-hearted day- and night-time sessions, but I have never really understood rock fishing. I do not believe it is possible unless you actually live close by and learn about the times and tides and all the other complications that go with them.

It was a light-hearted venture. A yearning for fresh air and exercise and an excuse to leave the womenfolk alone to shop and gossip as they are apt to do. We took our rods and an assortment of lures, plus a few frozen 'launces', which I suppose is the local name for sand eels. If it is not, then I really don't know what 'launces' are. They look like sand eels.

Drang, they told me, is another word for drain, and Canker Drang is a narrow gut between two massive rocks through which the sea fairly rips at full tide. As the tide covers the area and the Drang fills up, so (in theory at least) do the fish move in. It is a difficult piece of water to spin, and tales are told of expensive spools and lures being collected by the locals from the rocks at low tide when visiting anglers have had problems the day previously!

My American weedless lures with their brush-off spoon attachments, however, scraped their way back through and across the underwater snags without any trouble. They did not bother with too many fish either—but at least I had no problems.

Luggy decided, eventually, that spinning was a waste of time and that baits were called for. Here again, I learned a little wrinkle I had never known before. How to attach a dead sand eel so that it looks alive. It is a simple enough idea, which involves a long-shanked hook and a couple of half-hitches in the line, but, because it puts a bend into the sand eel, the action beneath a bobbing, swirling float is incredibly lifelike. No doubt regular rock fishers will have known exactly about the method for years, but to me it was something new that I thought might well be adaptable for pike fishing in rough water in winter.

Luggy always liked big floats. Even his tench floats in our youthful days were as big as salt and pepper pots, and the one he lent me today was no exception. About as big as a tennis ball.

It bobbed around in the surf, backing up under the rock where I was sitting, and occasionally I could see the sand eel wriggling furiously some 6ft below it in the clear Cornish sea. Something, I felt sure, would nail it before long and, just before darkness fell, something did.

The float dived under so incredibly quickly that I could not believe my own eyes, but just to reassure me it set off in exactly the opposite direction to which it should have been heading. I grabbed the rod, which was now firmly wedged between two pieces of rock, and wrenched it free. Forgetting all about the slack, I swiped at fresh air, missed, cursed and swiped again. The clutch gave a short protesting squeak and, remembering all I had been told about keeping fish coming in these conditions, I began to try to crank some line back on the spool.

From then on, events happened rather quickly and powerfully. Something on the other end pulled for the open sea, almost ripped the powerful 11ft rod from my hands, surged towards the surface of the water 30 yards out, and left me bewildered and breathless looking at a straightened hook!

It is debatable whether it was a monster bass, a big pollack or a more run-of-the-mill conger, and no one will ever know. It matters little anyway, but it would have been nice to have seen what it was. Our total catch was two small pollack and, having filletted them for tea next day, Luggy and I spent a few hours with the 'launce-hook'. At low tide we went down on to the sand and began scraping around with these instruments, actually feeling for the sand eels beneath the surface. It is a tricky business and one that calls for speed. Immediately the hook contacts one of those quicksilver creatures, you have to run your finger down to the hook and pin it firmly into the bend before dropping it into the bait bag. I contacted several but failed to put one into the bag. Somehow they were always too quick for me, and I laughed loud and long at my incompetence.

There is undoubtedly a lot more to rock fishing than is immediately apparent, and Luggy thought perhaps we ought to try beach fishing for a change. So, with borrowed tackle and advice from Luggy's friends, I tried my hand at beach casting. The 'sea', I was told, was about right, and the bass ought to be in. Night time, they said, would be best, and 100 yards ought to be far enough out. You can just about hold with a 3oz pyramid if you get out past where 'it breaks', and if you don't get 'sanded up' you'll be O.K. with 18lb test line.

It was all mumbo-jumbo to me, of course, but I learned eventually that you had to cast out past where the first breaker showed, and that the tackle would remain stable there and bites could be felt. Getting 'sanded up', I understood, was having your lead buried under about a foot of shifting sand and being utterly and completely snagged beyond redemption. It actually happened to me and now there is no doubt. Of course, it happened on one of the very few casts I managed to execute past the breaker line. I have learned to expect and accept such things when I try anything new, but it was very difficult to come to terms with those great chunks of lead and 12ft heavy-duty casting rods. For years I had not held a rod weighing much more than a few ounces, and it seemed a clumsy hit and miss affair to me, but I readily and hastily admit that it was only because I did not understand it. I could appreciate what was involved, even though I did not know enough about it to understand and practise it.

I lost about enough lead to cover a fair-sized church roof and eventually left the others to it.

The rest of the night is yours, I told them. You can have the rocks and the sand and that blasting fog horn that sounds every minute or so. You can also have the bass you are not catching now, and which I doubt very much if you will catch before morning!

So while I slept (still hearing fog horns and watching breakers in my sleep) the others fished on and caught bass up to 8lb 2oz! The best catch from that tiny beach for over twenty years!

The only other fish they managed to catch were wrasse and tiny pollack, but I was not concerned, since I prefer having something inedible on the end of the tackle to having nothing

167

at all. I know no one rates wrasse very highly, but at least they put a bend in the rod, and, given only a short fishing period, I decided I would rather hook something a little inferior than wait for a bass that didn't show.

So I crept down one of the easier rock faces next day and sat a spell in the afternoon sun, not caring much one way or the other. I had a few bites, caught several wrasse and tiny pollack and generally enjoyed myself.

Had I really wanted to haul in fish, I could have taken a charter boat out to one of the deep marks and caught pollack. I had done it before, but had always been conscious of the fact that the boat skipper actually caught the fish—not I. All I ever had to do was put the bait over the side (bait supplied by him, of course) and crank the fish up when I had hooked them. Had I been given the task of doing it alone, I would not have known where to start, and that thought has always taken away much of the pleasure of boat fishing for me. I know it is fun, and I know there are times when a knowledgeable boat angler will beat a novice over any mark, but finding the mark is the most important factor, and because I could not possibly do that under my own steam, I do not get quite so much pleasure from charter boat fishing. I recalled the good days when I had caught mackerel on a little 2oz fly rod and compared them with days spent hauling up pollack from the deep, and I didn't care any more.

All I wanted to do, and in fact all I did for the most part, was sit on a rock, kick off a few limpets for bait, cast out and relax. I caught few fish, it's true, but at least there were no telephones, and I was in no danger of being run down by passing juggernauts. In fact, I spent most of my time watching guillemots and oystercatchers. Their movements were much more graceful than the snooker-ball-sized monstrosity someone had loaned me to use as a float.

APRIL

In April I think of the March winds that always arrive a month late and storm-tossed boats and white bass and popping bugs and trout . . . and of Arkansas and the American spring.

F.J.T.

Poppers

My reservoir trout fishing is very much chuck-and-chance-it, but even so I still do not fare too badly. I have seldom been able to cast to an individual fish that I could actually see, however, and that's what makes me feel very vague about it all.

I have drifted around in a boat and located fish rising, of course. And I've cast to a rise with occasional success, but I could never say for sure that the fish I caught was the one at which I was pointing!

One of the best evenings I ever had involved a great deal of drifting and the boat-stalking of a number of fish rising to sedges. It was a bit like fishing with floating crust for carp really. There were these big fluffy moths on the surface, and every so often one of them would disappear with an almighty 'cloop'. I'd pick up my fly, change direction and drop it somewhere near where the last action had taken place. Then there would be a noisy rise in the spot where it had been previously!

Between two of us, however, we had eight fish before it grew too dark to see. We looked for a similar rise several times after that but it did not materialize until a couple of seasons later. Then, when it did, by some strange twist of fate we had no big dry flies with us. I did have some American popping bugs, however, and although these wooden-bodied little lures look like nothing on this earth, living or dead, the way they can be put to use is remarkable.

They can be twitched and made to make strange glugging noises on the surface, and they have the added advantage that they cannot sink. Big dry flies can be twitched and made to behave like fluttering moths by beating the rod butt occasionally. The trouble is that this invariably causes them to become waterlogged and sink. No such problem exists with the popping bug. Whether the trout accept them as insects or not it's hard to say but, occasionally, when there is surface or near-surface activity, you can put these little poppers to work.

The beauty of it all is that, if you're in a lazy mood and do not want to keep extending yourself casting, you can chuck the little monsters out and let them lie, giving them a twitch every now and then. Do not expect miracles, of course. There are times when they do not work because the trout cannot see past some other abundant food source. But do not write them off either; they can be incredibly effective.

I doubt if you can buy them over here, but it doesn't matter. With a piece of balsa dowel and a whisp of feather, you can make your own. It doesn't have to look good; it has to behave noisily.

I remember once using one on a private stretch of river where I was not restricted but given the go-ahead to use whatever I liked. On the day in question there were several accumulations of minnows near the surface, and every so often rainbows would rip through them, sending them in all directions. Had I not known trout were responsible, I would have believed pike were on the prowl. I caught two of those trout by letting a little popper float downstream over them and then drawing it back upstream against the current. I have no doubt that I could

170

have achieved the same, or better, results by casting a streamer upstream and whipping it back down faster than the current, but I used my own tactics because all the activity was near the surface.

Those are but two occasions when I have made the bug work: one a genuine 'rise-to-the-fly' situation, the other a 'strike-at-small-fish' situation. About as different as chalk and cheese, but the same 'fly' did for both of them. All the fish involved were rainbows and, while the chances are that it could be made to work in other conditions too, I somehow cannot imagine a brown trout falling for a popping bug. And here is an interesting fact. I have caught a great many rainbow trout, supposedly feeding on minnows, but I've yet to find a minnow in any of them. On reflection, I have, once or twice, seen the odd dead minnow floating off downstream after an attack by an aggressive rainbow and I wonder.

Do rainbows kill minnows just for the hell of it, or do they eat them? It sounds, probably, like a stupid question, but facts are facts. Other anglers have had the same experience. Did the rainbows I caught on the bug strike out of aggression or a need for food? I will not argue too much one way or the other, because I am certain someone could come up with proof enough of rainbows eating minnows. Sam Holland of Avington said to me once that if I was ever in doubt I should take a bucketful and toss them into his stews!

Nevertheless, on a river, where I have never seen a rainbow with minnows inside, I have seen a small brown trout containing seven!

And is there much difference between a roach fry, a stickleback or a minnow? No one could deny that reservoir trout exploit sticklebacks and roach fry, or that flies tied to look like them are deadly. Perch-fry flies were once pretty deadly at Hanningfield, and it was not uncommon for those who knew the fishery well to catch big trout on floating fry-type flies. Another situation where the popping bug might have worked.

Whatever the situation, it obviously helps if you can see trout exploiting a food source, but on big stillwaters it doesn't happen very often. When it does, I believe that the finding of the trout is often enough to ensure the capture of some of them. I do not believe it is always essential to imitate whatever they happen to be taking. It may help if you can recognize a particular situation, of course, but I am not at all convinced that it is necessary to offer the corresponding artificial when a rise is taking place. Sometimes it pays to be stubborn and offer something entirely different. I hope one day to work a popping bug on the surface during a general hatch—just to see what happens.

I do not need telling, of course, that the entomologist's approach will, over a season, prove to be far better than any of my outlandish ideas; but I never was much for going by the book. I believe there are times when it is possible to irritate rainbows into striking like pike, and a popping bug is the ideal 'teaser', as I have proved often enough.

The P.S.B.

Catching rainbow trout, fish that are artificially bred and introduced to waters where the possibilities of spawning and reproduction are known to be precisely nil, could hardly be regarded as the epitome of angling achievement. Yet there is something rather special about the rainbow, irrespective of the method used to bring about its capture. Satisfaction comes with contact, excitement comes with the acrobatics that usually follow, and a sense of achievement comes only when the fish is on the bank. That, when a bait or spinning rod is involved, is a pleasant and enjoyable kind of fishing, but it lacks magic. Magic comes with the use of a fly rod and, lest you should put me down for a purist fly fisher, let me say that my knowledge of entomology is limited and my fly casting, compared with that of many anglers, is atrocious. That is why I prefer rainbows to browns. The rainbow, because of its aggressive nature, may be teased into taking weird-looking artificials that really bear no resemblance to anything living in or around the waterside.

For years I followed the doctrine of those who tried to 'match the hatch', and it is true that in the process I caught some

172

biggish fish, including a brown trout of 5lb 13oz. I believed that in order to catch rainbows from big, deep, still waters, it was necessary to 'spoon them out', sort out their disgusting stomach contents and try to find something similar in my fly box. It worked often enough, and I'm quite sure that there were days when a strict imitation worked better than a chuck-and-chance-it streamer; but then I began to think more deeply.

If I caught my first rainbow of the day and found out, by inspection of the stomach contents, that it had been feeding on, say, some kind of green nymph, in theory I believed I ought to select an artificial green nymph as near to it as possible and fish it hard all day. They're 'on the green nymph', I'd say, and those other anglers who believed likewise made the necessary changes themselves.

Then it occurred to me that I had, in fact, proved only that *this particular fish* had been feeding upon green nymphs. There was nothing to suggest that *other fish* were behaving in a similar fashion. And following this line of thought to its natural con-clusion, I wondered why, since the fish had been 'on the green nymph', I had ever managed to catch it at all, and why it had taken the big bucktail I had been dragging along the bottom!

I would never write off the chances of improving my catch by fishing as nearly as possible to a general rise, but, to prove a point, I have deliberately fished on and caught just as many fish with big wet flies while the surface has been literally boiling with activity. I won't say it was any more pleasant or that it gave me any great sense of achievement, but it proved a point I have always believed to be true. There are several main sources of food available at the same time in most waters, and, even when it appears that every resident rainbow trout is feeding upon one special fly, nymph or other waterborne creature, there are more exploiting the other, unseen sources. Thus some trout settle down to become bottom-grubbers, while others become fry-chasers and insect-feeders. No single food source could support them all.

Such is the temperament of the rainbow trout, however, that it can be completely distracted from its chosen food source and

FJT with an early catch of rainbow trout

stimulated into attacking a fast-moving lure fly, a fly-spoon or even an acrobatic jig. It is its aggressive nature, I'm sure, that makes a big rainbow chase and attack a twinkling bar spoon. I do not believe the spoon resembles any natural item of food or that the rainbow accepts it as such. I believe it nails it out of sheer irritation. Or contempt.

Up in the Rocky Mountains of the United States many years ago, I fished for the rainbows of the clear mountain streams. They were not big fish I sought (a pounder would be above average), but they were, in the main, very free risers. The little white coachman would come bobbing back downstream in the broken water and suddenly disappear in a shower of spray as some hidden fish broke clear of the surface in its eagerness to take.

Standing knee-deep in the icy cold water, catching fish before making breakfast over the campfire, was an experience I shall never forget. Nor shall I ever forget the day when I failed to catch my quota and was greeted on my return by my completely inexperienced friend who had already begun dressing six beautiful pan-sized fish! That was bad enough, but when he showed me the monstrous, brightly-hued horror that had accounted for them, I simply could not believe my eyes. 'Trout do not take such diabolical creations,' I howled.

'These did,' he replied smugly.

A flash in the pan obviously. It could never happen again. A case of beginner's luck. The 5ft fly-leader was adorned with a $\frac{1}{32}$oz jig, the head of which was fluorescent pink, and the tail of which comprised a $\frac{1}{2}$in-long bristle of white hair. It had been trimmed off short so that it looked like a miniature brush. In later years, in fact, it became known as the P.S.B., or the pink shaving brush.

I told the story a hundred times, I even kept half a dozen of those jigs in my box for over six years. I brought them out for laughs on the banks of the famous River Test and displayed them in fishing lodges around America and Britain. Not once did I, or any one to whom I showed them, consider trying them.

Their concentrated weight at the end of a fly line would have made them almost impossible to cast, and that, plus their ghastly colour, made a joke of the whole situation. But wait!

On a private and exclusive stretch of chalk stream in Hampshire, I saw a big rainbow lying deep in over 10ft of water. It was hugging the bottom and nymphing with monotonous regularity. In that fast current and with only a floating line, even my copper-bound nymphs could not get down. The keeper suggested I pinch on a big shot and *lower* the nymph down, but fly fishers do not normally carry split shot. I had none, and I was frustrated.

Looking through the fly box I saw these six P.S.B.s, laughed out loud and, without further ado, tied one on to the leader. I did not cast, but simply flipped the rod over, allowing the jig to enter the water with a 'plip' and sink immediately in front of, but at least 3ft away from, the nymphing rainbow. What happened then really startled me. There was a blurred flash of movement, the pink spot disappeared completely, and the rod was almost pulled from my grasp. I had no need to set the hook; the trout did it for me. The water exploded some 10 yards upstream as the rainbow trampolined and shook its head angrily. It had taken the jig in anger, I'm sure; now it was just as angrily trying to rid itself of it. I will not bore you with a lengthy account of its capture, except to say that when weighed later it just touched the 5lb mark. The jig fell out as I put the net under it!

That day, with a keeper just as intrigued as I was, we took another six rainbows. My limit was eight fish, but that lure proved so deadly that I developed a conscience long before I had taken half a dozen. Only at the insistence of a friendly keeper did I continue to fish. But it proved a point and taught me the lesson to beat all lessons. Never believe it is essential to imitate the food source of a rainbow trout. Never accept the fact that rainbows are not feeding. They do not have to be. They can be caught even when, to all intents and purposes, they are fast asleep!

Since those days, I have truthfully lost count of the number of rainbows I have caught on jigs. I have, where allowed, tried fishing them on an ultra-light spinning outfit, but, although some kind of success rate has been achieved, it is nowhere near as high as that achieved with a fly rod.

Jigs are *not* easy to cast any great distance, and their continued use completely ruins a good fly caster. The technique is different. 'Ungainly' is, perhaps, a good description of the action needed to achieve more than 20 yards, but it *can* be done. The advantages of using a fly rod lie in the ability to keep in touch with the business end of the tackle.

Holding a fly line between thumb and forefinger, retrieving in short bursts or figure-of-eight folds, bouncing the bottom and putting action into the jig with the rod top, all make for a better understanding of *how* and *where* the jig is working. Direct line contact is so much more positive than that through the many angles of a spinning reel.

The correct action of a jig, as salt-water fishermen know only too well, is an up-and-down motion. At the extent of a reasonably long cast, this action has to be achieved by sharp pulls on the line and an occasional lift of the rod tip. As the jig draws closer to the rod, the action needs to be decreased slightly so that the up and down movement keeps within a 12in limit. This, like most forms of still-water trout fishing, is not selective. It involves continual casting, retrieving and searching, but most takes are very positive. The exception is when a trout takes the jig 'on the drop'. After missing on the upward lift, a rainbow will occasionally upend and take the jig while it sinks. This will not be felt at the rod end until the lift is imparted again, by which time the trout may have rejected the lure. A fleeting pluck is often the only indication felt but, if the speed and action of the jig is increased, a second take may well follow.

In small, clear streams, where rainbow trout can be seen lying deep, half hidden by weed or basking just below the surface, the reactions of a rainbow confronted by the non-stop motions of a dancing jig have to be seen to be believed. Many a big fish lies under bank cover or in the shelter of overhanging trees or bushes. Casting to it is next to impossible, but a jig lowered into its direct window of vision (or, if its head is hidden in cover, as close as possible to its tail) will usually bring about some kind of violent reaction. Obviously stealth and concealment are essential, and, if the fish is not alarmed, the chances are it will 'attack' the jig as soon as the up-and-down movement is imparted. The kind of smash hits that only rainbows can deliver demand some kind of insurance against breakage of leader. This is extremely close-range fishing, and it is essential to hold a few feet of slack line in reserve. Too much slack, however, may catch up in bankside herbage and do more harm than good.

Sometimes, the entry of the jig will cause the trout to bolt in apparent alarm, and one is led to believe that an earlier experience is still remembered. Patience will sometimes pay just dividends in this situation, however. The jig can be left lying on the bottom until the rainbow returns to its lie (which it will often do within a few minutes). Then, if it is lifted *slowly* in front of the fish's nose, it may well be taken with unbelievable aggression. Or, if the trout panics again, a complete change of lure colour may then bring about the desired result.

The only other reaction likely to be experienced is one of complete and utter indifference. The trout may back off slowly, sidestep and return to its original position, or it may simply stay put, refusing to move unless actually *touched* by the jig.

It is fascinating and frustrating to sit over a big rainbow and work the jig a few inches from its nose with no reaction at all. But it is encouraging to remember that, for no apparent reason, after an hour's futile fishing, the trout may begin to liven up and move towards this offending, insignificant intruder upon its solitude. One second the trout is languid, the next it is trying to imitate the tail end of a tornado.

No self-respecting brown trout could ever be conned into such behaviour. Only rainbows could be made to react so decisively to such torment; which is one reason why I regard them as rather special. Fishing for them this way really *is* magic, and results speak for themselves.

Beaver Carp

I pinched a piece of new white bread on to the hook, flicked it out with the light spinning rod and watched it sink slowly under its own weight from the stern of the moored houseboat.

It was April, and I was on Beaver Lake, Arkansas. The sun was high, the bass were 'off', and I was at a loose end. Or at least, I had been until someone had mentioned that there were carp in the vicinity. Then I had lost interest in bass and had exchanged my weedless jig for a baited hook. I had done so because I like to catch carp anywhere and because I believe that carp are grossly underrated by American sport fishermen.

Each time I visit the United States I try to convince my

many friends there that carp really are worthy of study and pursuit, that they are remarkably easy to catch and that they put up a fight that is comparable, pound for pound, with any fish that swims.

I can claim a modest success with carp in waters as far removed as Michigan and Oregon, and I am happy to say that I can also claim a number of converts to carp fishing. That, I feel, is really something in a land where carp are looked upon as vermin. This Arkansas venture, I thought, might prove to be another opportunity, but first of all I had to prove whether the carp were real or imaginary.

I leaned the rod against the rails and began edging my way round to the cabin for a cold beer and a comfortable seat.

I never made it!

The rod tried to jump the rails as something took hold of the bait and made off at high speed. The tip thumped down towards the water, the butt end lifted, and the whole outfit started to slide overboard. I dived, grabbed the handle, and hung on just in time to save the rod, but too late by far to connect with the fish responsible. It had long since departed, but at least it seemed that there was nothing imaginary about these carp!

I re-baited and cast again, this time holding the rod and letting the line rest lightly between my thumb and forefinger. The new bread sank slowly and even before it had reached bottom I felt the line tighten and run out. I eased off fractionally and struck hard and far back to set the hook. Something on the other end took off for Missouri, and I held on as hard as I dared, but being forced to give line time and time again against those powerful runs.

It was exactly fourteen minutes by Bill Hughes' watch before we slid the borrowed salmon landing net under that carp. During those fourteen minutes a small crowd had gathered to watch, and, while I played the fish (or the fish played me— I was never too sure), I was conscious of the conversation going on around me.

I heard someone say, 'The Englishman's tied into a big old

bugle-mouth.' Another said, 'He's sure got to wrastle that baby.' And yet another remarked, 'I never saw a bass put up a fight like that.'

I was using a line of 6lb breaking strain, which probably accounted for the time it took to land the fish, but even taking that into consideration, I think it was a fair example of common carp power. It weighed 14lb, and a minute per pound seems to me to be about as much as you can ask from any sporting fish—salmon included.

Several hours and thirteen carp later, I found myself talking to a very interested group of fishermen. They were mostly bass and crappie men and included at least one professional guide, but they had undoubtedly acquired a new and sudden interest in the carp they had ignored for so long.

Bill Hughes, a fly fisher of repute and a man with nothing good to say about bait fishing, expressed a desire to catch one, and, within minutes of casting, he had himself latched into a fish of about 15lb. He called it a 'horse', perhaps with some justification, for it was indeed a powerful fish.

Others followed suit, and for the rest of my stay on Beaver Lake I preached the carp gospel and described English carp-fishing methods to this group of new enthusiasts. It was not a novel experience to me, and I was not in any way surprised to see this sudden interest develop. It had happened before in the United States, and I am human enough to admit that I have been rather pleased and proud to find myself the tutor in a land where I am almost invariably a humble student.

But the average American angler, who would not bother to walk half a block to fish for carp, still finds it hard to believe how highly we rate ours in Britain.

Those Arkansas carp were ridiculously easy to catch. They were eager biters, and the only skill lay in handling them on light tackle. They were strong fish and, like all the other American carp I have caught, streamlined, fully-scaled and fast. But I had plenty of room and plenty of time. There were no snags, and I could always afford to let the fish have its head. That is part of the fun of carp fishing in the United States. You

FJT with Bill (Goat-head) Hughes and a catch of carp from Beaver Lake, Arkansas

can often take them in open water and have a straight man-to-fish fight without having to 'horse' them out of snags, stumps or brush. This means that finer tackle can be used with a great deal more finesse and general enjoyment.

Later that month, in Illinois, I fished for carp with a young American whom I knew simply as Rod. I never got to know his full name but, as he was a carp fisher, we had a lot in common. In the heat of the late afternoon we were fishless and biteless. The carp were 'off', and the only activity on the lake came from a dozen or so ducks 50 yards along the bank. A woman appeared, carrying a bucket; she nodded to us briefly as she passed, and began tossing pieces of bread to the ducks. There was much quacking and squabbling for a bit, and then all went quiet again. Some of the floating bread portions drifted down to where Rod and I were fishing, but we hardly noticed them. We were half asleep anyway!

Suddenly there was a swirl on the surface, and a piece of crust disappeared with a noise that I can only describe as being like porridge going down a sink! I knew English carp liked floating crust, but this was the first time I had seen it taken in America.

Rod sat up with a start, and I motioned him to stay quiet. We were concealed behind some tall rush cover, and the carp were obviously unaware of our presence.

'Now,' I said, 'I will demonstrate to you ye olde English art of margin fishing. Before you know it I'll have these carp eating out of my hand. This is the first time I've been able to meet 'em on my own terms!'

I showed Rod how to fix up a margin tackle, and we both poked our rods out over the water so that the crust-baited hooks hung vertically from the tips and rested on the surface. I pointed out that no line whatsoever touched the water, so that the possibility of a carp fouling it and becoming alarmed was completely eliminated. We sat back and held our breath as a dark shape approached and began to swim round Rod's crust. A big mouth opened, the bait disappeared, and the line tightened. As he made to grab the rod, I held him back briefly and was about to tell him that there was no need for haste, when the whole outfit launched itself into the water and disappeared! Rod stood there wild-eyed and amazed, looking at the spot where his rod had been a second before! He didn't speak, probably because he couldn't. And I felt very small.

It had been my fault entirely. Rod was using a multiplier and I had forgotten to warn him that, since this was exceptionally close-range fishing, he should leave some slack line on the bank. I was using my fixed spool reel with the pick-up off and that problem would not have arisen for me.

Rod had good reason to be sore at me. My smart-Alec idea had cost him a complete outfit, but he was strangely silent. I think he had been stunned by the speed at which it all happened.

There was a happy ending, however. We rescued the tackle by casting around with a big treble until we picked up the line. The rod was dragged ashore and, by a sheer miracle, the carp was still attached. It was a tired fish and had little to say for itself at that stage, but it made me feel better! Rod started to talk to me again too!

We probably didn't deserve that eight-pounder, but at least it serves to show how remarkably effective margin fishing can be. A letter from a mutual friend later informed me that Rod had got the hang of it and was doing great deeds on his local waters in Indiana.

One day we hope to carp fish again together, and I hope it comes soon.

Doddy

Down in Cornwall I watched the old bass fisherman on the rocks. His tackle was crude, his bait a strip of fish, and, as he cast out into the surf, I wondered if he was fishing seriously or if this was just an excuse to be out on a fine day. It was April and, in my view, too early for bass off the rocks, but then I am no expert at bass fishing. I only knew that the locals told me it was not worthwhile starting until the middle of May and since I've seldom caught bass from the rocks before June myself, I was prepared to believe them.

But to satisfy my curiosity I went down to see the old bass fisherman. I felt almost as if I was trespassing, for it seemed that this particular rock was his private preserve. Old Doddy always fishes there, and I don't believe I have ever passed that spot *without* seeing him.

No, he told me, it was not too early. He had, on occasions, caught bass here in March and, come the middle of May, it should be good fishing again. Meanwhile there was always a chance, and he intended to make the most of it before the happy holiday-makers came!

Not that he had anything against holiday *anglers*, he told me.

He would, if he could, help anyone interested in any kind of rock or shore fishing, but he couldn't abide those who came with their airs and graces but little knowledge of fishing, to slaughter fish unnecessarily.

In the past, he said, school bass, immature fish weighing less than 1lb, had often been killed and left to rot on the rocks because they were unwanted. The same thing happened to the mackerel year after year, and it was time the holiday anglers realized that you couldn't go on for ever taking fish in large numbers.

Doddy is the kind of angler I admire. He has little in the way of fancy tackle and wouldn't know how to use a great deal of it if he had. His old wooden centre-pin reel and his long cane rod are kept serviceable, and he knows how to handle them both despite their weight. A modern fixed-spool reel would never be part of his armoury—nor would an ultra-light, hollow glass-fibre rod. Doddy has handled them both and doesn't rate them at all.

'You can't wind in a big bass and lift it up these rocks with one of those "peel-offs" (meaning a fixed-spool reel),' he told me. And, having seen how essential it is to keep fish on the move once they're hooked here, I see his point.

The area he fishes is deep and turbulent. There are hidden rocks and great masses of weed to foul the line and help a hooked fish to escape. Once the tackle is caught up in such places there is no alternative but to pull for a break. If you can keep a fish coming from the very second it is hooked, the chances are that it will have no opportunity to dive for the sanctuary of the rocks or weed; but you can do this really well only with a centre-pin or multiplying reel. A direct-drive reel allows you to wind against a fish trying to take line; a fixed-spool reel does not. It demands a pumping and winding technique, which, irrespective of how skilfully it is executed, often allows the fish a brief second's respite. And that is all it needs.

Doddy was talking mainly of bass, but he has taken big plaice from the same rock, and he told me that the technique was much the same. 'Crank 'em in,' he said. ''Tis the only way.'

He has caught a good many bass weighing over 10lb but prefers the two- and three-pounders to eat. And, despite his knowledge of the rocks and his opportunity to reap big harvests when the fish are really going, Doddy never does.

'There's plenty of fish for everyone to have their share,' he said. 'But if we all catch them unnecessarily when they're easy, the day may come when there'll be none at all. I catch enough for my own needs and a couple for my friends. Then I pack up and go home. There's always another day.' There is great wisdom in the old man's thinking. It would seem that there is no bass shortage in his part of the world so far, and he believes that if all bass fishers had held similar views and had practised their own 'personal conservation policies' during the past ten years or so, there might have been no shortage elsewhere.

We hear of alarming shortages around other parts of the coast, and those who are genuinely concerned have tried very hard to preach a gospel of moderation. But not everyone agrees with them. Those anglers who look forward to an annual bass harvest argue that their catches are nothing compared with those taken commercially in trawl nets and on long lines. They believe they are entitled to their catches.

I wouldn't know the rights and wrongs of it all, but I reckon both sides might learn a bit of a lesson from old Doddy.

We talked on into the lunch hour, and I could have listened to him all day since so much of what he said made sense, but I had to go elsewhere, and I left him in peace to watch his big red-topped float bobbing up and down on the waves.

When I came by again two hours later Doddy was about to leave. On the rock lay a solitary bass—about 3lb as near as I could tell.

'There's still an hour of daylight left,' I said, 'and now's the best time for bass isn't it? Why not stay on a bit?'

And Doddy replied, 'I came out to get a fish for tea and I've got one. If I fancy one tomorrow I can always come and get another.' And, of course, I understood.

Here was a man who practised what he preached, and I admired him for it.

MAY

In May I long to return to Minnesota, and I think of blue herons and frogs and bluegills and crappie and beaver dams and loons . . . and of England's River Test and trout and tench awakening and carp and the building of the cabin on the Ouse.

F.J.T.

Minnesota Bonanza

Brother Ken and I lay on our bunks listening to the pounding of torrential rain on the cabin roof. Thunder cracked and lightning bolts hit the far shore of the lake where we were encamped; sleep would not come. We had jetted to Fargo, North Dakota, by way of New York and Chicago, we had back-tracked the 70 miles to Dent, Minnesota by road, and we were tired. It was not the jet-lag that kept us awake, however, nor was it the noise of the storm; it was the made-up tackle in the corner and thoughts of the fishing we were about to participate in that kept us tossing restlessly.

At three o'clock in the morning the storm abated, and a ghostly moon tried to ride the still-angry clouds. A gentle snore came from the direction of Ken's bunk, and I became certain, there and then, that I would greet the dawn with sleepless eyes. Once Ken begins to snore all is lost. . . .

But suddenly there was a pounding on the cabin door, and Jack, our host and guide, was bawling us out. I blinked in the morning sunlight as he yelled, 'You guys still sacked-out? Move your butts, grab your tackle, breakfast's cooking and the fish are biting.'

We moved our butts and grabbed our tackle!

Breakfast of bacon, eggs, pancakes and toast was washed down with hot coffee, and, in less than half an hour, we were catching fish from Jack's boat on Big McDonald Lake.

It sounds, perhaps, a little too good to be true, but the term 'catching fish' means literally, and very honestly, catching a fish at every cast. I have never known its like before or since. For sheer *numbers* of fish I have yet to find a water to equal it. And the exciting part about it all was that here all methods were permitted. There were limits, of course, but since those daily limits were more than we would ever need, they were quite irrelevant. What pleased us was that we could use bait rods, float tackle, light-spinning outfits, jigging gear or fly tackle with equal effect.

The lake is big, deep and clear. Much of it is quite barren and characterless, but here and there green bulrush beds surrounded by anaemic-looking lily pads are present in shallow parts. Fallen trees, stumps along the shoreline, and weed beds comprising curled pondweed are recognizable fish-holding areas, but the real hot spots are those known only to Jack and anglers like him, who have, over the years, found and marked them well. Reefs and drop-offs they are called, and whether they are located by plumb-line or transistorized sonar, they are the answer to every angler's prayer. They are jealously guarded, and marked only by prominent land features. Buoys or cork-markers would advertise their whereabouts and result in their becoming 'fished-out'.

Jack had located perhaps twenty such spots in a ten-year period, and he was wise enough to know which ones to visit on a given day. At the end of the week I might possibly have been able to locate one of those spots fairly accurately, but I am still vague about the rest. In order to appreciate the fantastic quality of the fishing, I must explain that we all three fished at some time during each day for food. Limits of thirty bluegills, twenty crappie, eleven walleye, eight pike and six bass per angler were on the cards, though highly unlikely. Legally, our boat could have taken three times those numbers, though in the case of all but the first two mentioned species, such a feat would have been nigh impossible. Nevertheless, bluegills were there a-plenty and crappie too if they could be found. To catch one particular limit of bluegills took me twenty minutes. The whole episode was timed by my two companions who left me to it and, since I kept only those fish that were above a self-imposed size limit, I undoubtedly caught more than half that number again.

On that occasion, as on many more, I used float tackle, a 9ft, light, soft-actioned rod and a grain of sweet corn. I cocked my float with a weighted jig hook with the barb flattened. There was a reason for this. Bluegills, when in feeding mood (which is nearly always), are quite suicidal. They'll swallow hooks as large as size No. 6 quite easily, and the disgorger that will allow them to be unhooked and released has yet to be invented. The loaded end of a jig hook prevents gorging, and makes for quick and easy removal.

There were times when it was necessary only to lower a jig with a white, yellow or pink 'skirt' over the side of the boat to catch fish. Mostly they were small, but every third or fourth fish would be a 'keeper', and one in every twenty would weigh in the region of 1lb. The fishing was such that we were often all three into fish at the same time, and Ken and I quickly learned to tie in a short piece of heavier line between our jigs and reel lines. Those 6in of 6lb monofilament meant that we had a hook link stronger than the rest of our tackle. With our short, jigging rods held high, we could reach down and *lift* out our fish on the heavy link without putting strain on our fine reel lines. It saved a great deal of net wielding, kept us out of each other's way and speeded up our catch rate.

This was fast fishing, but it was slow compared with that we experienced on the day we set out with fly rods only. Working the shoreline and casting to within inches of the bank for any-

American anglers fish for food; here one demonstrates how to fillet at the waterside

thing that happened along, we were suddenly all three into big bluegills. Our popping bugs had hardly touched the water when they disappeared. What we had located was a huge spawning area, with the big male fish standing guard. These brightly-coloured, orange-throated fish were not strictly feeders. They were sentinels, striking at anything and everything that dared to encroach upon their territory. Our insignificant pieces of cork and hair could not be tolerated by the outer guard. They were attacked without mercy—and each attack resulted in our adding yet one more fish to our tally. In just over an hour, without extending more than 10 yards of fly line, we took 300 fish, averaging perhaps 8oz each, with many over 1lb. Then we called quits.

From that catch we had kept our limit of thirty for food; the rest had been returned, and it is quite possible that some of them were caught again as they returned to the redd.

Enough was enough. It was great fun but all too easy, and we moved on to pastures new. Through a narrow, shallow channel we dragged boat and motor into what appeared to be a small isolated lake. A secret area, an unfished water. Hidden by trees, cut off by the almost dried-up channel, it was heavily weeded and looked to be different from the main body of water. Ken fished deep with a blue and silver jig as the boat drifted wherever the breeze took it. I cast a big black lure-fly towards the shoreline or any other likely looking 'structure'. Jack fished a small wet fly. It was an immediate anti-climax. The water seemed dead, and Jack was about to gun the motor when Ken's rod bent. Bass? Crappie? Northern pike? We had no idea, but we would never have guessed it to be a catfish.

Weighing nearly 3lb, a brown bullhead came sullenly to net after boring deeply and becoming weeded several times. It was an excellent specimen and unusual too, since these are usually only caught on bait. Good to eat, the bullhead is a bottom-feeder and is sought eagerly in parts of the United States by night fishers. I have breakfasted on them many times in the West, but I have not seen a bigger specimen than Ken's.

I tossed my fly idly towards a shallow, sandy bank, began to strip back slowly and felt all go solid. I thought I was snagged and that the drifting boat was pulling my rod top round, but I was soon to learn differently. The water boiled, and a fish moved swiftly towards me. 'Bass,' said Jack. 'Take up your slack quickly or you'll lose it.'

I stripped in line, lifted the rod and felt a pleasing tightness once more. Bass are occasionally acrobatic and spectacular, but they submit quickly under pressure. This was a four-pounder—just—and, since we had not eaten bass on this trip, we kept it to fillet later.

With little more than half an hour of daylight left we chose to turn for base, but not before Jack had tried an exploratory cast towards a particularly thick weed bed. His rod arched, and, without yet having seen his fish, he remarked, 'Now that's what I've been trying to find—crappie.'

It was a two-pounder and the weed bed was fairly crawling

with them! In that last half hour of daylight we accounted for over ninety fish. They were fat and full of fight, but, oddly, none weighed as heavy as Jack's first fish. Most would have turned the scales at the 1lb mark; very few were under it.

We had no need for any more food and so returned them all, marking the spot well for another day. When we *did* return, however, it was to find that the crappie had stolen silently away to some other hunting ground.

We never found them in that lake again, and for the rest of our stay we fished purely and simply for fun. We trolled for walleye, jigged for sunfish with many coloured coats and waded deep with fly rods to catch bluegills, crappie and small bass.

When light-hearted bets were laid as to the first limit bag taken, I thought to speed up my rate of catching by using a team of three flies. I ought to have known that cheats seldom prosper! It is *not* easy to play three bluegills at a time; it is even more difficult to boat and unhook them! I tried it several times but in the end I realized that I was putting myself at a dis-advantage. Nevertheless, there is something very pleasing in the feel of three positive takes on a fly rod.

Our week ended all too quickly, of course, and soon we were on our way to Arkansas to fish for carp, bass and catfish. But that's another story.

Willie and Wink

The pleasant'st angling is to see the fish
Cut with her golden oars the silver stream,
And greedily devour the treacherous bait.
            William Shakespeare

Most times when I go fishing in the United States my timing appears to be wrong.

'You're just a mite too early,' they say. 'Next week, when the water warms a little these bass will be hitting like crazy.' Or they'll say, 'What a pity you weren't here last week. Those bass were fairly tearing up the shad shoals on the top and we had a ball.'

191

Always, I should either arrive yesterday or tomorrow to get the best sport, but I have never taken too much notice of these tales of top-water fishing. They remind me of the tales I hear of evening rises on the trout reservoirs. I think they are pure fiction, or at least reserved for everyone else but me. I have yet to see them and I tend to be sceptical.

When 'Wink' Winkerman told me that he would show me some top-water bass fishing one morning, therefore, I was polite without being over-enthusiastic as I promised to be ready to go at six o'clock next morning.

The door-bell chimed in the distance, and I heard but did not heed it. It somehow formed part of my dream, and I turned over to continue it. It was a musical and pleasant chime, not an ear-shattering alarm bell, so I carried on dreaming.

The bedroom door burst open. Bill Hughes roared, 'Get your butt in gear, Limey. Wink's here and we're late.'

I got my butt in gear (whatever that means) and, still half asleep, piled into the car. We were at the Rocky Branch boat dock by the time I had awakened properly.

I climbed into the bass boat, stepping gingerly among a snarled-up heap of multi-hooked lures, zipped up my anorak and sat, back to the bows, as Wink roared across Beaver to a spot some 5 miles distant. It was a somewhat nerve-shattering experience, bouncing across the top of the waves at that hour of the day, and I thought to myself that if there were any bass near the surface to begin with, they would be unlikely to stay there for long with all that noise. It was cold, too, but Bill and Wink did not seem to notice.

Suddenly it was not cold any more and suddenly, too, the water was still and smooth. We were out of the main body of the lake and in the lee of a big bay, the margin of which was a mass of submerged, dead trees. Wink cut the motor and all was peaceful once more as we drifted slowly over the calm surface looking for signs of fish.

Bill pointed to a spot some 20 yards away where an area of several square yards looked slightly different. The water was dimpled or riffled as if a slight breeze had disturbed it briefly, but looking closer I could see a dense shoal of tiny fish priming. 'Those are the shad,' said Bill. 'Now watch what happens.'

I sat and watched, forgetting that I wasn't even tackled up yet.

The surface erupted as a largemouth bass ploughed through the shoal. Then another and another. Wink's lure flew out to the spot; Bill's followed a split second later; and I began frantically threading my line through the rod rings! I learned, and I learned quickly, that you have to be keyed up and ready when the action starts. There are only a few seconds in which to reap the short harvest before the bass go down again. There then follows a lull while the shad shoals reform. When they do they are usually a long way from the original spot and it is then that the fun begins. It is rather like chasing shadows. You switch on the silent electric motor and try to sneak up on them, but while you are doing so the bass tear into another shoal somewhere else. You look around to find it is the spot you have just left, and you realize that had you stayed put you would have been right in there with them. But, of course, if you wait they never come. It is reminiscent of stalking carp with floating bread crust. You see a carp 10 yards from where your crust is lying and hastily recast to it. At that precise moment there is a slurp in the spot you have just vacated and the loose piece of crust left behind disappears down an even bigger carp's gullet! It seems that fish the whole world over are just the same.

That is more or less how it proved to be on the day in question. We caught a few nice bass, but it seemed that the majority of them stayed out of range or moved in to feed the moment we left. Those we caught were full of fight, though none weighed more than about 2lb. They hit our hollow-nosed plugs as if they really meant it, and when they hit, they hung on as if surface plugs were going out of style.

At one stage Wink and I saw a 'rise' simultaneously, and we tried to beat each other to the punch. Wink's lure landed a foot to the right, mine a foot to the left—but it was Wink's rod that bucked a split second later as the fish hit. It was a white bass, strangely enough, a fish we had not really expected. Wink reckoned that my lure riled it and that it turned on his out of sheer cussedness, but I think it was the luck of the draw. We had fun nonetheless, and the few fish I caught gave me a lot of pleasure. I have caught more and bigger black bass in other places but usually in deep water on jigs and plastic worms. Top-water fishing was very exciting to me, but I realized I had a lot to learn before I became proficient.

We explored a number of bays and inlets during the remainder of the morning and picked up an odd fish here and there before the activity ceased altogether. Then the rain came. It did not last long but the heavens fairly opened, and, but for the shelter of a tiny, privately-owned boathouse nearby, we would have had a real soaking. Just as quickly as it came, however, the storm passed, and we had begun to make our way back to the boat dock when I saw some surface activity in the distance. Excited now, I yelled 'Bass—over there' and Wink swung the boat over to where I pointed.

Great fish rolled on the surface, and I began casting to them frantically. It was some moments before I realized that Bill and Wink were not following suit. They were enjoying a private joke at my expense, and the laugh was certainly on me.

'You'll see what you're casting to in a minute,' Bill said. And I did. Suddenly I caught a glimpse of one of these great fish and I'll swear it was 4ft long. 'Gar,' said Wink. 'They don't hit lures as a rule but some people fish for them with hookless lures made of unravelled hemp rope. Their teeth get caught up and they can't escape. Could be good fun I guess.'

I didn't have time to do anything about it then, but I still have the thought in mind.

The Cabin and Peace
From a May Diary

Do we not all, at some time or other, feel the urgent need to escape somewhere and do our own thing for a few days, a week or even longer? Most of us can compete with pressure, but our reactions to it are possibly different.

I have friends who, following an earthquake, hurricane or shipwreck, would sit down, fill a pipe and set to thinking out the way round it. I have others (like me), who hit the panic button, rant, rave, stomp their feet, threaten all kinds of dire actions and usually do precisely nothing about it when the mower won't start. There are times, however, when it is important for me to escape from people and places. To write as I want to and not to a deadline. My retreat is perfect.

Our old fishing cabin lies three fields over from the nearest farm track and a long haul from the nearest road, and I have spent most of the day listening to the thrush on the roof. His song is just as Browning described it so many years ago:

> *He sings each song twice over,*
> *Lest you should think he never could recapture . . .*

All day he has sung his song, and, although it is now no longer April, which was the time Browning longed for, this late May thrush is with me still as twilight falls. Incessant, nonstop, glorious. I have listened so long and attentively that my writing has suffered severe lapses. It was the need for silence that drove me to this very spot, but with the bird songs come other compensations. Here there are no phones, no petrol fumes, no radios, no lumbering juggernauts; just fields, a few cows on the other side of the river, the sound of a tractor chugging over a distant hill. And me and my scratch pad. I have allowed myself one luxury—the cassette recorder is softly playing country music in the background. It's the only kind of music I appreciate; the only kind I've ever liked from boyhood. It is simple and uncomplicated, as a countryman himself should be.

There are memories built into this fishing cabin, which is still as sound now as the day we built it something like twenty years ago. We (Dick Walker, my brother Ken and other willing helpers) built it to an architect's specification (raised on concrete pillars about 2ft 6in above the ground), and we completed it in the three months between the closing and re-opening of the coarse-fish season. We worked only at weekends, and it so happened that every one of those weekends remained dry. We were never 'rained off'.

We dug a 6ft-deep cesspit, we poured concrete by the ton, we levelled and bevelled, and we drank a lot of tea in the building of this cabin. Dick's twin boys learned what swear words were all about and began using them even in places where they didn't belong, but it did them no harm. We grubbed out brush and slopped creosote and paint around like they were going out of style. We called in cousin Joe to tile the roof. 'Green tiles mind,' we said. 'None of those red things that show up for miles.' We built in bunk-beds, piped bottled gas to various lighting and heating points. We even built in a sink, despite the fact that we expected to haul water from the river. But the friendly farmer had other ideas.

'It's all down hill from the house,' he said. 'If you'll pay for the pipe, I'll mole it in across the fields and you'll at least have "running cold" if not "running hot"!'

He took the pipe across a derelict canal on the way, and we had running water from the day we declared it open. We were supposed to have had a separate meter, but it never happened that way.

Everything about this fishing cabin has been good, and all my memories of it have been pleasant. Problems there were in plenty at the beginning, but none that could not be resolved by thought, genius or sheer blind luck.

The concrete came ready-mixed in an enormous tanker that ground its way slowly across the track. It had to cross the canal on the way, and the little hump-backed bridge didn't really look capable of taking it.

'That's all right,' said John, the farmer. 'I've tested it to eleven tons.'

'Good,' said the driver. 'Trouble is, this beggar weighs fourteen!' He made it to the site, unloaded and then promptly stuck half-way back with an empty unit. It took John's crawler tractor about a minute flat to straighten it out.

We, meanwhile, had to work feverishly before the wretched concrete started to 'go off'. We had plenty of time, of course, but ready-mixed concrete is usually delivered fairly stiff, and it was no joke running back and forth to the river for water. But we were younger and had great visions in those days.

We had never heard of Milton Keynes, we had never seen a dredger, we had no reason to suspect that out lovely rented stretch of river would be abstracted, dredged and almost completely ruined in twenty odd years.

They tried to ruin it about ten years ago and didn't quite succeed. So now they've had another try. When I look at the spot where the otters used to play I feel sad. When I see how the bank cover, despite promises to the contrary, has been hauled out, and when I look at the few meagre inches of weedless, reedless water, I wonder why any fish in its right mind would want to stay in such a place.

But there's more to a fishing cabin than fish, and, if I'm truthful about it, the very fact that it was built ensured that our fish catches became fewer and less spectacular, even before the desecration.

We grew older, we grew softer, we grew more mellow. We realized in due course that we no longer had to prove to each other that we could catch chub or roach or dace or perch or pike. We had done it so many boastful times before, and on an icy winter's morning we would find ourselves wandering back to the cabin instead of fishing on hard as we'd done in the past. Suddenly the thought of freshly brewed tea, a warm by the gas fire and a short session of telling lies seemed to be much more important than yet another 4lb chub.

In a way, this cabin spoiled us. It made us into men of little courage or faith. The first hint of snow, sleet or hail sent us scurrying to its shelter. Our all-night sessions seldom lasted all night because we knew there were four warm bunk-beds waiting for us when we'd had enough. And it was strange how we all seemed to decide we'd had enough at about the same time. The fact that we usually spent the rest of the night talking and brewing tea probably didn't really count for much.

It is a fact, you see, that the company you keep is of much greater importance than the catch. We look forward to meeting up with good friends and spending a day in their company. If a few fish come our way in the course of a day, so much the better; but it really matters very little.

And I cannot deny that this cabin has found me many friends. It also found me a lovely grandchild. My daughter and some friends spent a holiday in this very spot many years ago, and some of our young fishing friends came to view the prospects at the same time. Perhaps they knew something? The outcome of it all was that Ian and Valerie met, married and gave me Avril, the greatest joy of my life.

It is dark now. The bird songs have ceased. The countryside overtures are at rest, which is a good enough cue for me to join them. There *is* peace in this world somewhere; I have found it here. I hope I always will.

Luck

The old station-wagon fairly ate up the miles from home to Hampshire. The roads were dry, there was very little traffic, and the warmth of the early sun made itself felt through the window. The stereo cassette recorder was playing soft country music, and the singer was complaining that 'it only rains on me'. I knew today, however, that it would not rain on me. Today was my first day of what I regard as trout fishing proper: weighted nymph fishing on a small chalk stream stocked with big fish.

I had risen early. There had been no need for an alarm call since the blackbird in the may tree outside my window had already greeted both me and his whole immediate world, urging us to wake up and revel in a morning as glorious as his own magnificent voice.

I might not catch a fish, but at least I would be free to do my own thing: to creep and crawl the overgrown banks, to spot a fish here and there and to hope to outwit them all when the time was ripe. If I failed, it would be my own fault, and not that of another thoughtless angler walking the bank. Today would be my day; I did not have to share it with anyone else unless I wished to do so, and circumstances had prevented my partner from joining me.

How different this fishing is from the other kinds I have practised. I rarely fail to catch fish from this stream, but I sincerely believe it would not disappoint me if I did. I have had lean days but, in all the years I have fished there, have had only one complete blank. I sometimes become angry because I fail, but the anger is at myself for doing something utterly stupid and spoiling my own chances. I may become frustrated at my own inability to put my fly or nymph where it ought to be, but I am never despondent. The nature of the water and the surroundings are such that there truly is 'more to fishing than catching fish'.

Once upon a time, when someone quoted those words to me, I put them down as an excuse for failure. Today, having caught easy fish so many times that I have tired of it and sought more difficult methods, I recognize the truth in those words.

Every year I have a surplus of trout, and, as I have lost count of the number given away to friends and colleagues, I believe I am entitled to be philosophical. My pleasure comes from the whole operation and not only from catching fish. Even the drive down is a part of it.

At the side of the road a big dog-fox lay dead, hit by a fast-moving car or lorry during the night. Three carrion crows lingered near the carcass, possibly having second thoughts! A magpie crossed the hedge to my right and I bade it 'Good morning, Mr Magpie'. Everyone knows it's bad luck not to be polite to magpies, and it would be a great pity to spoil such a marvellous day. Three young rabbits scuttled away as I opened the big barred gate to drive along the track. Two hen pheasants pecked away unconcernedly on the grass verge. A cock bird strode arrogantly in front of the car as I approached, and I slowed down to let him cross.

I parked on the rough gravel patch by the stream, poured a cup of coffee from my flask, took it to the little bridge and drank of it while I looked into the sparkling water. This is what my trout fishing is all about. Not for me the wading and casting into the murky depths of a reservoir in the early season. That can be pleasant enough in summer, but I have no wish to join the annual race to grab the best spots and compete with others in what appears always to be a long-distance casting event. I find enough competition from the fish, and if you should perchance remark that I am not skilful enough to execute long casts with a shooting head anyway, you would be right. I never made any claims that I was.

I had recently opened a letter from my dear old friend Ted Trueblood of Idaho. In it he had said, 'I don't have to prove I can catch fish, nor do you, and, like you, I'd rather do the kind of fishing I enjoy.' He was on an entirely different tack, but the principle remains the same. Ted can cast a fly a very long distance with great accuracy but, like me, he derives pleasure from spending time in beautiful places and believes that catching fish is only a part of the scene.

Today I refuse to be half-frozen to death trying to fly-cast in a March blizzard, and I will not allow myself to be pounded to pieces on an exposed boat in an April gale. I have done it and have not enjoyed it. I spent some time once in Ireland fishing with Fred Buller on Lough Mask. I did not catch anything of note because I fished only on the pleasant days. On the days when the fishing was reputed to be at its best, I refused to leave the shore. I had had one dismal experience of being half-blinded by spray, windswept, cold, miserable and bone-shaken on a day that had made both local and visiting anglers wax enthusiastic about prospects. These were the conditions when the trout would respond, and if trout were to be caught at all, today would be the day, they told me.

Fred, a very close friend, found it impossible to believe that I wasn't enjoying every golden moment of it! And I, in turn, simply could not believe that anyone could claim the slightest enjoyment from taking such punishment. Unless, of course, the catching of the fish constituted the *only* pleasure. I would rather not catch fish in a pleasant situation than catch a sackful in an unpleasant one, and I simply cannot imagine that I would ever be able to pay attention to any of nature's other wonders while struggling to survive, to remain seated, to handle fly tackle or even to see through drenched and dripping spectacles. Undoubtedly some anglers derive pleasure from such conditions. I am pleased that they do but, thankfully, I do not have to join them.

The clear water rushed under the narrow bridge. Odd pieces of ranunculus swirled in the eddy formed below it, and a raft of floating weed had gathered on either side. It was not the best of fly-casting places, but I was in no hurry. Something would show soon I felt sure; meanwhile I assembled my tackle.

My leader was a short, seven-footer with no knots, and I tied on the weighted shrimp pattern that had proved so successful in the past. I make no claims for its creation. Dick Walker tied the original; my brother Ken copied it. It can, however, be quite deadly and, in a situation where there is no indication of a hatch of any kind, it is one of the best patterns I know.

Three dark shapes moved in the turbulent water, dropping back, edging sideways, moving up and vanishing from sight with no obvious set pattern. One looked to be about twice as large as the other two and, since there was no way of being selective, I chose to fish from downstream and cast into the general area.

It is not a precise method of fishing and it really demands the attitude of a salmon angler in that it is necessary to be persistent and cover the water systematically. A rainbow's reaction to the shrimp usually coincides with the precise moment of 'lift'. The shrimp is allowed to sink, line is drawn in to keep contact, and then the rod is lifted in order to make the shrimp rise in the water. (There is another technique involving an across cast that causes the line to tighten downstream and bring about the same effect. Dick allied this technique to his shrimp dressing successfully for winter grayling some years ago.)

My situation was different, however, and I had to induce the lift myself. I did so hoping to catch one fish, and was prepared to accept the smallest of the three graciously.

Mine is a simple style of fishing, but there is a certain rhythm involved that is quite enjoyable. Each cast is an easy pick-up-and-shoot. There is need for only one back cast.

It was when I was almost completely committed to the back

cast that it happened. Suddenly I could not lift the line, the rod stopped with a sudden jerk, the water exploded, and I was almost pulled off balance as the fish made for the bridge. It could not have made a better decision from my point of view, and some ten minutes later it came to net, still trying to forge its way upstream. Had it turned down and used the current to its advantage, the tale might have had a different ending. Even so, it was very close. The hook pulled out as I lifted the fish clear.

It weighed $5\frac{1}{4}$lb, and was obviously the biggest of the three I had spotted.

Sheer luck had undoubtedly played its part. Everything had gone well from the word 'go', and you cannot ask for a better start than that. The rest of the day didn't matter any more.

The End of the Road?

'I once knew an old man who was very poor. He lived in a log cabin beside a rushing river. He could safely drink from it. There were plump, colorful trout to strike his fly. And across the river was a mountain. From his window, the old man could watch the deer and elk that wandered on it. Chipmunks played around his doorstep. Squirrels scolded from the pine trees that shaded the cabin. Grouse would often wander into his yard.

'When the old man needed groceries, he rode his horse six miles to town to buy them. His purchases were always modest; this was before the days of Social Security. He had to make his pennies last. But he had his cabin and his horse, and his dog and his garden, and the trout in the river, and he didn't really know that he was poor. If he could no longer roam the mountains and collect a rich harvest of furs from his traps, as he once had done, that was to be expected.

'But his friends at last convinced him that he was too old to live alone in his cabin, six miles from the nearest road. So he went to the city, where he had a daughter, and moved in with her.

'I knew him there as I had known him earlier in the mountains, where he had given me freely the hospitality of his humble cabin. And I saw him fail—day by day, week by week, and month by month. He lived less than a year in the city.

'America today is in grave danger of losing all of those intangibles that give life quality. When it does, I fear, it will die—like the old man.'

The foregoing words by Ted Trueblood, one of the greatest outdoorsmen of the American West, are the words of someone whose wisdom stems from age and vast experience. They apply, of course, to the world over and not only to the United States of America. If we do not heed them we shall all suffer the consequences, but how can we spread the message or convince those who do not care and never will?

By a strange quirk of fate the little poem that follows became adjoined to that part of the manuscript that contained Ted Trueblood's words.

Well they ruined all our rivers
Dried them up to tiny slivers
Running green and dank with dirt
And when we said how much it hurt
Us, well they didn't really care.

Well they filled in all our lakes
With all their filthy waste
Killed the fish, the reeds, the lilies,
And they told us we were silly
When we said they didn't care.

They started on the seas then,
And I wish that snows would freeze them
And the profits they are taking
From this hell on earth they're making
Just because they didn't care.

Before they've taken all the waters
From our sons and from our daughters
We must show them what they're doing
Can result in only ruin.
We must teach them how to care.

It was on a scrap of paper written by my daughter Valerie when she was young. Its message is as clear now as when she wrote it all those years ago, and I felt obliged, because of this strange and completely unplanned link between youth and age, to include it among these my thoughts for the future of our heritage.

It sounds very much like a direct steal from Kipling, and it possibly leaves something to be desired from a poetic stand-point, but that does not concern me one jot. Nor should it.

Perhaps I can take a little credit for making someone so young aware of what we are doing to ourselves; perhaps she discovered it through discussions with other people. That does not concern me either. I am proud that she had that kind of awareness, and I hope that her generation will be able to do something more about preventing our self-destruction. I doubt if it will, but I still hope. Despite their many mistakes, con-servationists of the United States of America have made some progress. Wrongs are still being done, but many have been righted. Perhaps there *is* a future. At least the steps taken in America may give us encouragement to fight. One thing is sure. We must never relax!

At the beginning of 1979, Arthur Oglesby, in *Shooting Times*, stated some hard facts regarding the future of Atlantic salmon stocks. He told how they were being affected by over-exploitation and called for an end to apathy on all our parts. Soon, he said, there may be no salmon left, and future genera-tions may never get to know what one looked like. I have no doubt at all that he is right, but, apart from raising a loud voice (to which the powers that be will not listen), what can we do about it? What action can we take to stop both worldwide and domestic over-exploitation?

As far back as 1969 I wrote in a London evening newspaper that the time was rapidly approaching when the Atlantic salmon would become virtually extinct because of disease and excessive netting at sea. I followed this by suggesting that a possible substitute might be found in the coho salmon, which could be established in some of our large inland waters where inlet streams would afford spawning facilities. The American authorities had proved beyond all doubt that the coho was adaptable, and both the U.S. and Canadian governments had worked together to transform part of the Great Lakes area from a disgusting health hazard to a sport fishery of tremendous potential. They had wisely looked upon sport fishing as an industry in need of a lift, and that once-depressed area is now, ten years later, a great tourist attraction, enjoying full employment and prosperity.

The coho story needs telling in detail for its incredible success to be understood, but though the choice of fish and all that went with it played an important part in the proceedings, I believe that the co-operation between two governments and

Bob Rankin, an American journalist with coho salmon freshly caught from Lake Michigan. We could learn so much from US conservationists

the realization that the creation of sport fishing was likely to provide the best return for money invested were the key factors. There has never been another success story like it, and we might do well to copy our American friends, not necessarily in the same kind of venture, but to prove that salmon fishing provides all kinds of revenue and employment. But how is it possible to put over this point of view when entire governments are dedicated (despite denials) to the banning of sport fishing altogether? Even in the event that the practical benefits to be derived from good salmon fisheries were at long last recognized, how is it possible to stop nylon netting on the high seas? How can you enforce laws upon commercial fishermen, who will always exploit to the full every possible source of income? How can you stop the reaping of golden harvests by those who will always continue to over-crop even though they know that to do so is eventually to wipe out their own livelihoods? 'If we do not have them, someone else will,' they say. And they are right. The result is a free-for-all, with everyone taking more than a fair share and devising ways and means of beating the system.

Nor does this apply exclusively to salmon. Human nature being what it is, it applies to all harvests. Not to take a crop is wasteful; to take too big a crop is utterly stupid, but this kind of action has been going on for years. It will continue until stocks are exhausted, and then another source of exploitation will be sought.

Once we had a thriving tunny-fishing industry developing around the north-east coast. It was a rich man's sport seemingly, but it provided work for charter boats, and tackle developments resulted from it. It all ceased when the Norwegian commercial fishermen moved in and wiped out all the tunny in the area.

Suddenly fox pelts have become valuable and thousands are being killed illegally by poachers who set snares indiscriminately for their immediate profit. Snaring is possibly the only way to control foxes, but if this kind of slaughter is allowed to continue, there will be none left to control.

A letter from my old friend in Cornwall tells of:

Bulgarian and Russian trawlers scooping up everything. We've had them again all last winter and all the Scottish and Hull boats (the last named who fish all night and catch far above their quota) take it to the Russian factory ships (twenty-five in Falmouth Harbour) and, if they don't want it, dump it there and then. No one seems to want to do anything about it. Next year the boats will be laid up, the crews on the dole, and there'll be a great outcry about the fishing fleets being let down by the government, the owners and Lord knows what else. I don't think I'd be too upset if the lot were drowned . . .

A typical example of a greed that is almost suicidal. And it doesn't take much effort to think up many more. The whales have almost gone, along with other creatures wiped out in the distant past, and one wonders how the seas will now cope with the food the whales *used* to eat!

Were it not for conservation methods applied to many kinds of fish and game, there would have been no next year's crop this century. Most rabbiters are wise enough to leave a few for next year's seed, but again, where profit is the name of the game, there is no thought for tomorrow. Another day, another dollar; another farm to work if this one fails to produce next year. And so it goes on.

'Ducks Unlimited' in the United States goes on producing duck for sporting shooters year after year at a cost that is possibly out of all proportion to what might be achieved by true control, but how do you control the numbers of duck shot in Mexico during migrations? Can you instruct a Mexican shooter to limit his bag, because the American shooter does? And probably more to the point, can you ask a salmon fisher, who possibly has but one or two weeks in the year to enjoy his sport, to return his catch because it is red and ripe with spawn? By some standards his big, red, old fish may be regarded as inedible, but he is legally entitled to take it back with him. Why, when hundreds of fish are being taken 50 miles from the mouth of the river he is fishing, should he not?

I have always thought the suggestion that it is unsporting to take a kelt, but acceptable to take a 'stale' fish a bit weird. I cannot see the sense of the laws that make it an offence to take a spawned-out fish. I've no wish to keep kelts, but I really do not see what good it does returning them. How many make it back to sea, much less back to the river for a second time?

Thankfully, although most of us would prefer to catch wild fish, trout conservation in the United Kingdom is probably the best in the world. Now that rainbows can be bred to grow to upwards of 20lb, and fish weighing between 2lb and 3lb put within the reach of everyone with a fly rod and a day in which to use it, pressures can be taken off natural resources. Thousands of escapees have found their way into rivers all over the country, and one wonders how long it will be before some of them migrate to sea and come back as fresh run steelheads. It *is* possible, I'm sure, and I have heard it said that evidence to support the theory has shown up in Scotland. Perhaps the day will come when rainbows discover the food not eaten by the whales and wax fat in the oceans. Then, I wonder, how long will it be before they too are over-exploited before returning to the rivers where they were released.

There is no stopping our foolish and greedy descent, nor will there be until it is too late. We send great jets into the air, each of which requires tons of oxygen to become airborne, and we cover our earth with a layer of smoke. We lay forests bare, we cover our seas with oil, and we break down our ozone with aerosol sprays. When our oil has all gone, and we are dependent upon the sun for energy, we may well be unable to go bare-skinned out into it. It's a gloomy prospect and there is no answer to be found because we are what we are.

Our apathy towards salmon conservation pales into insignificance by comparison, and we can only hope that our young anglers are able to do something about it. We have tried, but so far we have failed.

> *The reason for it all is that fishing is fun and good for the soul of man.*
>
> *Herbert Hoover*
> *30th President of the*
> *United States of America*